Pets in Particular

James Allcock

Pets

Pets in Particular

Introduced by Lesley Judd

James Allcock

Weidenfeld and Nicolson

*in association with HTV Limited and
Channel Four Television Company Limited*

To all the very good pet keepers
and may their numbers multiply

Published in Great Britain by
George Weidenfeld & Nicolson Limited
91 Clapham High Street
London SW4 7TA

ISBN 0 297 78923 6 Cased
ISBN 0 297 78942 2 Paperback

Printed in Great Britain by
Butler & Tanner Ltd
Frome and London

Contents

Introduction by Lesley Judd

What on earth is it about them that makes us put up with the hassle? – the extra shopping for a choosy palate, the constant mopping-up after muddy feet, the worry when they're ill, the panic when they're lost, not to mention those times when you end up on the floor while they recline in your favourite armchair! No, I'm not talking about husbands, wives or children. I'm referring to our national 'soft spot' – the family pet.

When the dog makes a snack out of the Sunday joint, and the cat goes to bed with a chop-bone on a pile of freshly ironed shirts, these are the moments when I yell 'Never again – no more animals in this house!' But I always relent, and the passing on of any of my animals has always been followed, after a period of sadness, by the arrival of a new four-legged source of joy and fury!

I can't answer for the rest of the pet-owning population but my reasons for continuing this love-hate relationship are well illustrated first thing in the morning. Everyone in our house will eagerly admit that I am not at my best at day-break, but when I growl at my family, bad tempered and bleary-eyed, the only one who does not growl back is the dog. It is Benji, our current canine companion, who accepts me 'warts and all', who's pleased to see me – even when I'm not pleased to see me – and who receives a pat on the head like others accept a knighthood!

My earliest memories are full of pets, real and imaginary. There was Bob, the dog who took the blame with me for trampling on my father's roses, and after Bob's demise (he was laid to rest under those very blooms!) I spent many happy hours pretending I was the owner of Rin-Tin-Tin – an Alsatian whose daring exploits featured on TV when I was a little girl. Since then there's always been a Maurice, a Brillo, a Benji or a Jo-Jo. Perhaps out of all of them Jo-Jo occupies the biggest space in my heart – well, she was an Irish Wolfhound and they don't come bigger than that! She was my companion during a particularly lonely period of my life, and I know it was mostly the need to keep her fed and exercised that kept self-pity at bay, and kept me fed and exercised as well!

If I had heeded W.C. Fields' warning about working with animals and children my career would still be struggling to get off the ground. As it is, I've always found both of these groups of diminutive 'co-stars' an excellent excuse to sit back and be entertained along with the rest of the audience!

Pets in Particular, my latest assignment, gives me plenty of opportunity to sit back and enjoy the animal antics while most of the hard work is done by the programme's vet, and author of this book, James Allcock. Apart from being a tremendous source of veterinary knowledge, James also has a 'lively' sense of comedy. I remember on one programme telling the viewers about my dislike of rodents, only to find James sitting next to me with a rat on his shoulder!

James has transferred his lively TV style into print and this is a book of wit as well as wisdom – though I must amend that famous old saying to 'Never work with children, animals or vets with a sense of humour'!

1 · *Why do we have so many pets?*

Napoleon said that England is a nation of shopkeepers. An opinion poll held today might or might not confirm this view. But if he had said a nation of pet keepers the poll would record an enormous 'Yes' majority, with a few 'No's' and 6% asking, 'Who is Napoleon? Is he in the charts?'

There is only one basic reason for the popularity of pet keeping: people *like* animals. Now that farming occupies less than 3% of the population, people find they need animals and that pets provide that missing animal contact for all the non-farmers.

Until the nineteenth century most animals kept by man had to earn their living in a practical way. Companionship was not enough. Dogs were valued as hunters, herders of cattle and sheep, or as guards to the family that fed them. This type of working dog had to be big enough to do his job. Cats controlled mice and rats – and in many cases lived on their prey and little else. A few bears, parrots and monkeys paid for their keep as animal entertainers working with human entertainers.

Yet a few animals were kept solely as pets, because their owners liked to have them about. The owner had to come from the wealthy ruling classes because no one else could afford the time or money to indulge in keeping non-earning animals. The history of many of the toy dogs illustrates this: the Chihuahua is believed to have been the sacred dog of the Incas; the Japenese Chin was a favourite of Japanese Emperors more than 1000 years ago, and the Chinese royal family insisted on a monopoly of owning Pekingese. Death was the fate of anyone who dared to steal these royal dogs.

Nearer to home, King Charles Spaniels tell their own story although an ancestor of this breed is said to have been a favourite of royalty before the reign of either Charles. After the execution of Mary Queen of Scots a spaniel was found hidden in her folded gown.

Certain cats were sacred to the Egyptians in the time of the Pharaohs, and they were definitely part of the domestic scene in the Middle Ages. They had weedled their way into a semi-pet status by Shakespeare's time. Shylock, speaking of 'A harmless necessary cat', suggests both the enjoyment of a cat's company, and its use as a pest controller. Where the witches' black cat fits in is not clear but these must have been pets, perhaps the only company for lonely old ladies shunned by all their neighbours, and only the cat cared if they lived or died. Just like it is in some modern cities.

9

Pet keeping as we understand it today started with the Industrial Revolution when there was a human population explosion in the manufacturing towns that grew up around 'those dark satanic mills'. Bill Sykes had his dog and Sam Weller's opinion about caged birds is close to twentieth-century views: 'And a bird cage Sir . . . a prison in a prison.'

Generations grew up without day-to-day contact with animals on the farm. So they took the scavenging dog – or more likely her puppy – and brought it up as a house pet. Cats became truly domesticated for the same reasons and I wonder how many pet canaries in the mining districts were the survivors from the birds that went underground to test the atmosphere. Wild birds were caught and caged to bring something of the country into the town, without much thought for the welfare of the bird.

Budgerigars arrived in the mid 1920s and, being the very fertile birds that they are, it did not take long before pet budgies were numbered in millions.

Jack Black, Queen Victoria's royal Rat Catcher was one of the first people to breed different-coloured rats and all the fancy rats kept as pets today are descendants of domesticated 'novelty' rats with a hundred years of breeding behind them. Now there are more than 6 million rats and as many cats, about 2 million budgies and large, but uncounted, numbers of gerbils, rabbits, rats, hamsters, terrapins, cold-water and tropical fish, to name but a few of the dozens of different species used as 'pets'.

'My pet' can be a term of endearment with implications of tenderness, although many husbands who hear those two words, spoken more in sorrow than in anger, know that they are about to be told something to their disadvantage. To be labelled a pet is not a guarantee that all will be forgiven whatever the sin, and labelling any animal a pet does not guarantee that it will always, or ever, receive proper care and attention.

Gooey sentiment has little place in proper pet keeping. Some of the most sensibly kept pets are those on slightly old-fashioned farms, owned by the sort of farmer who would normally be scornful of pet keeping. His dog might sleep on the chair because his wife allows it, but it just happens that his dog is a good dog with cattle, and given half a chance this farmer will enumerate all the virtues of the dog – and its mother, who's rather old now, so has a special box by the fire . . . I know a dairy farmer in Wales who has a small farm with about 20 milking cows, and rather more cats. When milking time comes around the cats are first in the queue and he fills their dishes from the first cow to be milked. Anyone hearing the farmer talk about these cats might gain the impression that they stole the milk; no one, farmer least of all, took the trouble to fill their bowls! And one assumes the cats themselves set off for the supermarket to buy the cans of cat food stacked in the dairy, charging them to the farm account.

To me, this is proper pet care; keeping an animal – or better still, animals in the plural – because you like having them about and you can give them a life style that the pet enjoys by having sufficient creature comforts with enough of the right sort of food and something to do all day. And never overlook companionship: either company of its own kind for the cats, or human attention enjoyed by the working dog, or the dog that lives in a house where people are about all day.

The English language is said to be alive and changing, and the term 'Companion Animal' was born some years ago to describe the animals that we keep, not for food or defined physical work but because they are nice to have about. These animals work by giving us pleasure and interest. This book is about Companion Animals in general and Pets in Particular.

2 · *Which pet?*

There is no one answer to the question, 'Which is the best pet?' because the answer varies with every potential owner. The best pet is the one that you suit, that you like and that you can provide and care for adequately, for richer, for poorer (because some pets are expensive to run) until death you do part. Pets are for ever and pets grow up.

When choosing your pet there is one great divide; those pets that can live with us in the house, and those that have to spend much of their life in cages or outdoors. Dogs and cats are the only true house pets, because they are the only two that can be reliably house trained. Budgies, canaries and the small seed-eating finches can fly around the living room and are much better for such exercise, although the picture rails and light fittings need extra cleaning as a result. Larger birds, such as mynahs which produce more semi-liquid by-products, would make any room uninhabitable in which they were allowed free flight. Monkeys, rabbits and bottle-fed lambs are equally unreliable.

So, if Group One is house pets, the choice falls between dog(s) and cat(s). Choosing one or more comes later but this decision as to quantity can affect the choice.

Let's start with one very definite statement about dog owning. ANY HOUSE THAT IS EMPTY FOR EIGHT HOURS PER DAY, FOR MOST OF THE WORKING WEEK, IS NOT SUITABLE FOR A DOG. It matters not how much you love dogs; no one can ask any dog to spend long periods of time day in day out doing nothing. In fact the dog does do things. He chews the furniture or the carpets. He barks or howls. The other alternative which is to let the dog roam the streets all day might be acceptable to the dog, until he meets a motor car, but packs of latch-key dogs are not acceptable, in town or country.

Someone at home for most of the time is a minimum requirement for dog owning. Of course there are exceptions when the dog can go to work with you, but remember that dogs live for fourteen years or more, and promotion, change of job or redundancy might mean that the dog's life has to change too. I receive a good many letters that start, 'Since I changed my job,' and go on '. . . so he has to stay at home and the neighbours are complaining.' So is the dog.

If you have the right home circumstances for a dog the next decision must be "which breed?" That comes later, but where it would be wrong to keep any dog it is quite possible to give a cat a satisfactory life. They do walk by themselves, they do their own things, they can come and go through a cat door and find feline company. Nevertheless every cat appreciates a routine and although he may be alone for hours at a time he expects his meal and your company at fixed and regular times. So if you are single with an active social life that means your home coming varies between 6 pm and 2 am from night to night – and sometimes out on the tiles all night – then your cat is going to be a very disturbed and confused animal. If he has any sense, as most of them have, he'll make friends with someone of more temperate habits and leave home, because you have failed him, it was wrong to choose a cat in the first place. Stick to goldfish in an aquarium.

Caged birds, and please note the use of the plural, fit into most households. They need a certain minimum attention each and every day, but if they are kept in the plural the daily timetable of feeding or cleaning is not important to the birds. Food and water are there all the time and they have the company of one another. A single bird provides excellent company for anyone who is house-bound, and the budgie has the benefit of human company all day.

Large birds such as parrots, macaws and even mynahs tend to be kept as solitary birds. The cost of buying the bird often dictates this solitary life but the bird pays in many cases. A pub parrot or pet-shop parrot has lots of things to occupy his time, the house one often has nothing to do, nothing to think about from morning until night – and is asked to live for years in such mindless boredom.

Birds have to spend much of their life confined in cages or aviaries and all the small mammals are also restricted to cages, hutches or runs for most of the time. Rabbits, gerbils, hamsters, rats, mice, chinchillas and guinea-pigs are the classic children's pets. If these little furry things are well kept they can teach children some very valuable lessons about life. About birth and sex; an explanation of the oestrus cycle in the hamster by a ten-year old can be an instructive experience. Small pets can teach responsibility. Mum has a critical part to play in this learning process. She must not take over when Ronald Rat or Gertie Guinea-pig has not been fed. She must be a fierce dragon and insist that care for others comes first, and just to emphasise the point, humans are not fed if their pets have been forgotten. The very small pets; gerbils, hamsters, rats and mice have limited life spans. Three years is senility, so their young owners learn that life is finite, death is its inevitable end. When that much-loved pet dies its young owner weeps, perhaps arranges an interment, complete with cross and flowers. Then, if he or she is a natural child, curiosity demands an exhumation six weeks later to see what has happened to the body. I don't think any of that behaviour is ghoulish, just educational and normal enquiry.

Small mammal keeping is not exclusive to children. There are many adult enthusiasts who breed and show these small animals and perhaps more who never think of showing because in their own mind they know that the best pair of rats on earth live in the cage on the sideboard.

If the conventional caged pets offer a wide selection of species the less conventional ones, so called exotic pets, widen the choice much more. However, DON'T, is the best advice to anyone contemplating monkey owning, or who would like to keep chipmonks, a mongoose, a coati mundi. There might be legal restrictions if the particular species is one to which the Dangerous Wild Animals Act applies.

Non-domesticated, exotic animals are very demanding of time, care and expertise in handling. None of these is cheap to buy, and beware of gifts. The gift monkey has probably bitten his owner half a dozen times and has some fairly repulsive habits as well. An advertisement in *Exchange and Mart* about ten years ago, before there were any restrictions by way of Dangerous Wild Animals legislation, illustrates this 'free to good home' problem where exotic animals are concerned. It read: 'Lion cubs, 6 weeks old, good with children and pets, £200. One-year-old lion (male), free to good home.' They grow, and depreciate.

All the pets so far have been warm-blooded ones. I'm not talking about the amount of affection that they show, but using the term in a biological sense meaning they regulate their own body temperature which remains constant within a degree or so ($101°$ F ($38·4°$ C) for dogs and cats, up to $107°$ F ($40·4°$ C) for budgies).

Fish, reptiles and chelonians (that's the group name for tortoises, terrapins and turtles), are cold blooded and their body temperature varies with the temperature of the surroundings. Low temperatures slow down all activity; tortoises hibernate; goldfish living in a frozen pond manage to survive but just exist in a torpid state, hardly moving and not feeding. Cold-blooded animals from tropical areas slow down if they meet a British winter (or some of our cooler summers) and slow down so much that feeding stops, and a progressive starvation starts. Correct temperatures are vital, in the real sense of that word, to cold-blooded pets.

It may be that the cold-blooded animals are not true pets, in that they cannot be stroked or cuddled as a dog, cat or gerbil can and they do not show obvious affection for their owners. There's no doubt that fish, snakes and tortoises recognise those who feed and care for them – and trust their keepers much more than they do a casual visitor.

All new-born animals are appealing and everyone wants to care for such helpless beings, particularly if they are orphaned. This concern is commendable and pet lambs, calves, pigs, chickens, jackdaws and monkeys live in the unlikeliest places. But they grow up. The playful lamb turns into a boring sheep. The calf into a heifer weighing half a ton at three years of age, and adult pigs are big too. Although such pets grow big they do not forget the human care and companionship that they knew when they were tiny. The sheep prefers human company to a flock of sheep. The heifer does not like the sight of a bull and the jackdaw, even when he is allowed to fly free, seeks human company and is accused of attacking children in the school playground when he only wanted to be with them. Hand-rearing orphans can produce misfits unable to integrate with their own kind. Look a long way ahead before allowing your sympathy to set off an impossible life pattern, allowing an animal to grow up thinking it is human.

Any babe brought up away from its own kind begins to believe that it is the same species as its companions. I know an emu that thinks it is a llama. It lives with llamas, eats hay from racks like llamas (not very successfully) but enjoys crushed grains as much as any llama. And there is a donkey, one of the seaside donkeys, that thinks he is a pony. About thirty donkeys and thirty ponies graze together throughout the winter. They are fed hay in racks in a separate paddock. Donkeys are called first for breakfast or supper and they trot briskly to start their meal. Except for one donkey who waits until it is the ponies' turn an hour later. His mother died when he was born and he was suckled by a pony mare that had lost her foal. Although there are donkeys galore that he could mix with, he prefers the ponies. Perhaps he feels they are a better class of equine.

The emu, the donkey, all those solitary ducks that think they are chickens because they came out of one duck egg amongst a dozen bantams, can continue an acceptable life in spite of the misapprehension. But the one that thinks he's human is rejected, lonely and miserable. If you rear orphans, keep them in very close contact with their own kind and while they rely on you for food, don't indulge yourself by making them rely on you for companionship.

Less than fifty years ago horses were working animals, on farms, in industry and commerce. Today ponies are nearly as numerous as horses were then but now kept simply for our leisure moments – a true 'Companion Animal' – not pets, and should not be treated or thought of as pets. Far too many ponies exist in misery because an inexperienced enthusiast becomes 'horse mad'. When the first novelty wears off the pony may be in a field several miles away. House-kept pets can bark, or miaow, if feeding time is forgotten. Ponies just wait.

If the right pet is chosen you'll both have a happy time, and enjoyable pets always receive attention – because that is part of the enjoyment.

3 · How many?

People need pets, and pets need company. The very best company is that of their own kind and there are very good reasons for keeping two or more animals together. This need not mean a breeding pair with all the happy results; the aim is company, not fecundity.

Company provides mental occupation and prevents hour upon hour of boredom with all the attendant behavioural abnormalities shown by solitary animals with nothing to do but eat and sleep.

Because dogs and cats live with us and are more or less free to wander at will, they can be kept quite reasonably on their own. Any cat with a modicum of initiative is going to find a friend over the fence – or with fire in his belly he'll find an enemy and overcome boredom by constant skirmishes. Dogs meet other dogs on walks, and yours and the dog next door might have a lot in common.

Nevertheless, two kittens are marvellous company for each other and while they are tearing each other to pieces those freshly embroidered chair seats are not being put to the claw test. Two cats will join together to protect their garden from invading cats. A couple of pups might be less destructive than one – for the same reason that saves the chair seats. It is much more fun to play with another living thing than destroy an inanimate object. If large breeds of dogs are involved, do remember that dogs grow larger and two fluffy St Bernard pups might fit the house and car when they are eight weeks old but at eight months they will need a larger hearth rug and overfill any car.

Caged pets almost always need company. Golden hamsters are the exception. They don't like other hamsters. I'm not even sure how they overcome this antipathy long enough to work on the next hamster generation. These pets like a life of seclusion and don't seem to mind overmuch if that seclusion is monastic. In the case of all other caged mammals and birds there are compelling reasons for keeping two or more.

Even the goldfish, all alone, swimming in constant sized circles around his bowl must feel that something is missing from his life and it would be nice to bump into another goldfish.

There is a social order, or pecking order if you prefer it, whenever a group of individuals live together. This order is determined by the animals themselves. Human interference is neither effective nor welcome. that does not mean that we cannot help sort out the occasional squabble but those snarls, snaps and quarrels are often necessary for one creature to establish his, or her place as boss of that particular territory.

When animals meet for the first time many of the troubles will be avoided if there is an honourable retreat available. Always provide hiding places. Plastic plant pots in a cold-water aquarium make a cave for a new fish to hide in. Place a box, or a brick within the hutch to provide shelter for a new gerbil, or rabbit and whenever possible always introduce caged animals to each other in a fresh cage. Thus avoiding the need to fight for familiar perches or territory.

In many cases two males kept together will fight no matter how long they have been together. Buck rabbits can suffer very serious injuries during fraternal quarrels and boys will be boys in the canine world, while 'cock-fights' explain the bird difficulties. Females are more pacific in most species so that an all-female group may be the only possible one unless a population explosion is accepted.

A peaceful time is more likely when there is enough space for any group of animals and more than enough feeding, sleeping and drinking places. Competition provokes quarrels. Birds fight for the highest perch or nest box – so if there are a dozen 'top sites', there are fewer squabbles. Quiet areas, so that a guinea-pig can sit and think (or just sit) without any disturbance from his companions, make for a peaceful atmosphere and plenty of food hoppers means that the shyest member of the group can still get a fair share of food.

As well as segregation of the sexes, embarrassingly exuberant reproduction can be prevented by neutering. (Embarrassing because even the most gregarious pet owner runs out of friends who would 'just love' a pair of gerbils, rabbits or guinea-pigs.) Castration of male rabbits, rats and guinea-pigs is a perfectly practical procedure. A fringe benefit of this operation is that the neutered male is less aggressive, both to other males and to his human owners. Buck rabbits in particular can terrify their owner by violent, and dangerous attacks with teeth and claws. Neutering of female caged pets is quite possible but very rarely undertaken. The wire barrier between them and any philandering male is an efficient contraceptive. When dogs or cats are kept in the house there are many more opportunities to find a mate, hence the desirability of speying she-cats and bitches to avoid unwanted litters.

4 · *Which dog?*

Dogs are unique, as any dog owner will tell you, but the special feature which no other species can match is their tremendous diversity in size. On one side of the scales, a Newfoundland, weighing 150 lbs or more and on the other Chihuahuas of about 2 lbs. Seventy five of the little 'uns to balance one giant.

Coat length and density extend from the near-bald Mexican Hairless through the short-haired breeds such as Whippets and, dear to my heart, Staffordshire Bull Terriers, to the fairly full-coated Samoyeds and Afghans, finishing with those covered with masses of hair such as Maltese Terriers, American Cockers, Old English Sheepdogs and the Hungarian Puli.

Shapes vary enormously. Dachshunds go for length and ignore height, while Irish Wolfhounds and Pyrenean Mountain Dogs are tall enough to wag their tails and clear the table. Pekes and Bulldogs can't poke their nose into anything and the very flat face does not always leave room for a full set of teeth (a pair of molars is omitted). Bull Terriers show what a Roman nose can look like and the extreme in nasal elegance must belong to the Borzoi. A breed that is somewhat aloof by nature, and who wouldn't be, with a nose like that to look down?

Ears stick up in the French Bulldog, hang down in the Cocker Spaniel and hang so far down in the Basset Hound that he can tread on them while walking. Tails curl forwards in the Spitz-type dogs, upwards in many terriers, lie straight behind (Pointers of course) or flow in an elegant curve. Man is vain enough to think that he can improve on Nature so he cuts the tails off many breeds.

There are black dogs, brown, blue, white, red and yellow ones plus a near-infinite mixture of these colours. Come to think of it there are no green dogs; perhaps enthusiatic breeders could aim for this and leave the tails as they are. The pups might prefer it and a colour change would not be painful.

There is plenty of choice in the physical appearance of pure breeds and they intermingle at times to produce cross breeds and add to the confusion. At present about 160 breeds are recognised by the Kennel Club and new ones keep cropping up – sometimes to the embarrassment of vets who don't always recognise this month's new model.

Appearances matter when choosing a breed, but even more important is the temperament of the dog and its activity level. Some breeds are very busy and want to be doing something all the time. Many of the terriers behave in this way. Working breeds such as Border Collies enjoy work and are bored if unemployed. Gun dogs were developed to spend their time with their master and go through thicket and water at his bidding. This 'busy-ness' factor is very important when fitting a new owner to a new dog.

One dog selection method is to relate dog size to house size: toy dogs for small flats; little dogs for maisonettes; small/medium sizes for semis; one size bigger for detached houses with a quarter acre, and the giant breeds for country mansions. However, this does not always work very well – dog should match its owner and family, not the house.

Many of the very big dogs are not busy. Bone idle could be a better description. Take a St Bernard twice around the block and his is tired out. I know an Irish Wolfhound, Pepper, living in a first floor flat in a converted Victorian house. The rooms are large so she is in reasonable proportion to the floor space, but when I was told by the couple who own her that they were looking for such a large dog I told them they were mad. I was totally wrong. She is well trained, she's been brought up to use stairs and accepts them as a normal part of life although her progress downstairs looks like a giraffe in difficulties. She has two short twenty-minute walks and one longer hour walk per day. If I meet Pepper when she is on her walk she sits down, and if I talk to her owners for more than two minutes she lies down – it's less effort than sitting. After her exercise she spends time watching the world go by, looking out through an upstairs window (elbows on the window ledge) and when this becomes exhausting she has a nap. Yet when she meets Georgina, my very busy Staffordshire Bull Terrier, playtime is boisterous to say the least, although George does most of the hard work rushing about. Pepper is just breathing a little faster when George is puffing and blowing like a steam engine.

These giant breeds learnt about energy conservation long before any adverts appeared in the newspapers. A hundred pounds of dog is not everyone's choice, and there are non-busy dogs in smaller sizes. The long-nosed breeds that were developed to chase by sight such as Whippets, Greyhounds, Salukis and Italian Greyhounds are 'explosive' dogs that take off for ten minutes of violent exercise at high speed, and are then content to relax for hours until the next explosion. They can fit very well into a busy human life.

Small dogs may be non-busy if only because short legs move many times to cover small distances, but they can be mentally busy and a bored small dog will yap for hours on end if he has to prove that his owner is not providing a very interesting life for his pet.

Dog keeping demands time and certain breeds need much more time than others. Short-haired dogs hardly need grooming; a polish with a duster once

A unique feature of dogs is their tremendous diversity in size. *(Below)* Sheep dogs are working breeds, and can be bored if unemployed.

a week is enough. Extra long-haired breeds such as Old English Sheepdogs, and even Afghans, which are not quite so hairy, can become a matted mess unless they are given several hours hard grooming each week. There are Cocker Spaniels with ears twice as heavy as Nature intended. The extra weight is dead hair, knots, tangles, brambles and sometimes a piece of chewing gum. Unpleasant for the dog and caused by idleness on the part of the owner who 'couldn't find the time'.

Many terriers need stripping, and Poodles and Bedlingtons need clipping. Arranging hair-do's takes time but they are essential if the dog is to feel comfortable and at ease with himself.

So step one in the choosing process is to decide the size, the activity level and the coat type that you are looking for. Colour is an 'also ran' at this stage.

Go to Dog Shows, just to look, not to buy. Get more than one dog book from the library. There are excellent 'Dog Directories' which list the virtues and vital statistics of every breed, although they tend to be rather reticent about any drawbacks. Talk to people with dogs. Dog deciding provides a marvellous opportunity to accost that willowy blonde with the elegant poodle, or, if your sex and inclinations dictate otherwise, the dishy young man with his Airedale. And the rather forbidding lady will be delighted to be asked and will extol the virtues of her Boston Terriers for hours.

Whether you read them or hear them, take superlatives about any particular breed with a pinch of salt. Breed enthusiasts can see no wrong in their dogs. They may criticise their children, husband or wife, but will never suggest that their breed is other than perfect. Everyone knows that Staffordshire Bull Terriers are without fault in any case – and I'm not prejudiced!

After deciding on the breed of dog, or even before, decide on the sex of your puppy. This should be a positive choice, not just what's left, or cheapest. Bitches may be a trouble when they are on heat, but neutering can solve this if you do not wish to breed from your pet and heats can be prevented or shortened by the use of hormone tablets or injections. An over-enthusiastic dog can be a trouble all the year round, but these inclinations can be controlled if necessary by castration if training does not achieve control.

My own preference is for a bitch, especially where children are involved. They are gentler, the maternal instinct extends to young humans and they are usually smaller which means that a toddler is not knocked over quite so easily as a result of canine over-affection. The wandering instinct is less prominent in the bitch. She stays home, waiting for the dogs to call.

Males are more aggressive in every species. Perhaps an advantage if one is looking for a guard dog, but the best protection and least worry comes from a dog that looks fierce, loves everyone and might lick a burglar to

Coat length varies enormously
from a Hungarian Puli (*above*), to
a short-haired Whippet (*below*).

death from sheer affection. More fights occur between dogs than between bitches, which gives another plus to the female, and bitches are cleaner around the garden. They do cause brown patches on the lawn when the grass succumbs to their watering but dogs are inclined to cock their leg on the cabbages, and even the door post in times of trial.

With breed fixed and sex decided, the next consideration is: Where from? There is only one answer: ALWAYS GET A PUPPY FROM THE HOME IT WAS BORN INTO. A change of home at seven or eight weeks of age is a stressful experience for any pup. If he leaves mother, after careful weaning, and continues to eat the same food that he ate with Mum, and goes to a comfortable new home free from any dog diseases then the stress is minimal and pup settles down without any hitch. But if he leaves home, goes to a pet shop or selling-kennels mixed with pups from other litters, each with his own variety of germs, and if there is a complete change of diet at the same time, and the kennel is colder than it should be, then there is a very high probability that the puppy will be unwell. At the best he might have a touch of infantile diarrhoea. At the worst he might catch parvovirus, distemper, kennel cough or an infantile diarrhoea that is serious enough to kill him. Because most infections have an incubation period, it's not possible to look at a puppy and say that he is free from any disease. If he has mixed with pups from other homes there is a chance that something is brewing. If puppy leaves a pet shop and goes to live with you he is experiencing his second change of home and diet within a few days. That could be too much – and when you find that out, it's too late.

Any puppy that leaves his mother and spends time in a pet shop or kennels before going to his permanent home might learn bad habits. Pup's mother is pack boss while he's with her and his brothers and sisters. She teaches him the rudiments of toilet training and teaches him that he is not 'top dog'. After a fortnight in kennels away from Mum a puppy will have forgotten any toilet training, he'll think that anything goes, anywhere, and it will. He may have become boss puppy, and be convinced that he rules the world. Re-training is possible, but it will take longer than in a pup coming straight from Mum and under your influence from the beginning.

Another reason for buying a puppy from his breeder is that you can choose *your* pup at an early age. I booked Georgina, the apple of my eye, several months before she was conceived. I met George's mother, Sheba, when I visited a kennel breeding Yorkshire Terriers. The house was full of tiny Yorkie pups and striding between them, like a colossus, was this ponderous Staffordshire bitch. She thought her name was 'Mind the puppies' because that was the phrase she heard fifty times a day. Sheba was (and still is) one of the most welcoming dogs I have met, but not in a violently demonstrative way. She sat at my feet and pushed her nose to be scratched, indicating that she was very pleased that I had arrived and as hostess it was her duty and pleasure to make me welcome. This, plus her solemn care for the tiny pups, sold her offspring to me before George was a gleam in anyone's eye. I am delighted to say that George has inherited all her mother's virtues.

By now some one is asking, 'Does he think that all the dogs in the world are pedigree? I prefer mongrels, much tougher and have nicer natures.' More than 50% of the dogs in the United Kingdom are pedigree. This means there are a lot of cross-breds, at least two million of them. I am not anti-mongrels but if you are starting with a puppy there is a greater risk of unexpected developments if it is cross-bred. Puppy might inherit the virtues of each parent, but there is just as much chance that it will collect all the vices. Ultimate size is an unknown (or less-known) quantity and many mongrels sold by pet shops or offered from Dog Rescue homes are 'father unknown'. The unlikeliest matings take place.

Bomber was the result of the union of a Bloodhound bitch and a Dachshund dog (belonging to the same owner so it was slightly proper). He looked like half of each of his parents, very long, very heavy with Dachs legs. I never thought of him as a happy dog, just too long to fit and the distance between his very short front and hind legs was so great that going up steps was very difficult because his front legs reached too far forward. The garden was on a steep slope, which explains a lot.

If you know and like the mother of cross-bred pups and she is the type that suits you, then choose one of her offspring. If you know father as well, and he suits, the risk of a misfit is very low.

As for mongrels being tougher, I don't think there is any difference except in those cases where a very weak pedigree pup, that Nature would not have allowed to survive, is reared by using everything modern science can offer – and a less than perfect pup will live to enjoy an imperfect life.

One final point to consider when choosing a puppy is life expectancy. The smaller dogs tend to live longer; fifteen years or more is the norm for little terriers, Poms, Pekes, and such lightweights. Spaniels, Labradors and Collies quite often reach fourteen. The giant breeds are old by the time they are ten and many do not make double-figure ages. Their lives are shorter than ours, but the Labrador puppy that meets your daughter from primary school could be the elderly dog that escorts your granddaughter on her first perambulator trip.

5 · The new puppy

Three decisions have been made: breed, sex, and background. Now we're off to collect the puppy. But which puppy out of a litter of four dogs and three bitches? And how old should he be when we do collect him (or her)? To avoid brackets galore I'll do as the lawyers do, and use 'him' to embrace 'her' from now on.

To answer the second question first, the answer is about eight weeks old. By that time a puppy should be completely weaned and independent of mother as far as food is concerned. If he stays with her and the rest of his siblings for any longer, he will grow up to behave as a dog in a pack of dogs – not the behaviour that one wants to see in a well-mannered pet. A pet dog has to learn to live with humans, to accept their wishes as law, to enjoy the company of other dogs, but with restrictions. This approach to life can be learnt very quickly, and painlessly between the ages of eight and twenty weeks. A puppy's basic philosophy does not change much after this age. The puppy that lives in a kennel with Mother until he is twelve weeks old will be much more difficult to toilet train. Mother teaches him that he must not soil his bed or feeding area, but everywhere else is available. The privacy and seclusion of his kennel is a poor preparation for an outside world of vacuum cleaners, telephone bells, noisy motor bikes and all the other musical accompaniments of city life which terrify some dogs, but other well-adjusted pets take in their stride.

When selecting, the 'middle' puppy is often the best one. The bold extrovert that pushes forward and chews your shoe is likely to develop into an opinionated dog, certain that he knows best and should have always his own way. A strong-minded owner will use his pet's self confidence to produce a dog that is sure of itself and quite convinced that his master or mistress rules the world, and his owner will enjoy this exalted status. A less strong-minded owner will find that the dominant pup grows up into a dominant dog that growls and snarls to get its own way.

The pup that hangs back and is not 'come hitherish' might develop into a nervous adult, inclined to panic and less easy to train because he is too busy worrying about everything else that is going on. Should you take that little one so as to be certain he has a good home? This is one occasion when there's nothing wrong in being single minded and selfish. You are searching for a perfect pup as your companion to live with you for a very long time. Forget the other pups, look for yours.

Now examine your final choice in great detail. Look for faults; you've already found his virtues.

Here's a check list, starting from the front:–

The nose should be moist and free from any discharge. Suspect any pup with a hot dry nose.

The mouth should look and smell clean and tidy. There should not be any excess saliva stuck around the lips. If there is, it's not caused by teething: eight weeks of age is not a teething age and pups hardly notice their tooth eruptions which start at about four months of age. The top and bottom rows of teeth should meet in a level bite, with the two sets of teeth just touching each other. (However, some of the flat faced breeds, Boxers for example, have the front teeth in the lower jaw protruding further than the upper ones).

The eyes should be bright and wide open with no signs of any discharge or excessive tears. The pupils should be equal in size and the whole eye appearance symmetrical. Some Collies have a 'wall' eye, where the iris (that's the bit around the black pupil in the centre) is white, while the other eye may be brown or grey. Sometimes both eyes are wall eyed. It is a normal happening and does not affect the sight in any way.

The ears: the skin inside the ear should be clean and smooth with no signs of excess brown wax. A puppy should not resent his ears being ruffled or start to shake his head after his ears have been handled.

The coat should be even with no bald or roughened patches. Look along the spine from the tail forward and push the hair forward in this area. You are looking for signs of fleas; either the insects themselves (as dark mahogany beasties, the size of a small grain of bird seed, flattened from side to side and moving about), or flea droppings (little black specks, looking like coal dust). Check for lice too. These are less common than fleas and may be found on the ears or around the neck. They are grey/blue in colour, again about the size of a grain of bird seed, and live attached to the dog's skin. Look at the skin on pup's tummy. It should be as smooth as that of a young human's rear, free from spots, scratches and blemishes of any kind.

The tail end should not be passed by with averted eyes. It is not indelicate to inspect this area. There should not be any signs of diarrhoea, soreness or redness around the anus. If the puppy has been docked, look at the end of the tail. Sometimes healing is not quite perfect and insufficient skin has been left so that the bony stump of the tail is not properly covered. Docking takes place before five days of age so that healing should be totally finished seven weeks later.

The legs: each foot should have four toes. The nails may be doubled – some King Charles Spaniels have this feature which may be accepted as normal by their breeder. Nevertheless, double nails can be a nuisance later in life and I would not buy a pup with such a defect. Dew claws, which are the equivalent of our thumb, lie on the inside of the front legs high enough up to be out of contact with the ground. These are often removed when the puppy is a few days old. If this has been done the scars should be totally healed. If the claws have not been removed there is nothing to worry about. Removal or not is largely a matter of fashion. Dew claws are sometimes present on the hind legs, although it is normal practice to remove these in every breed except the Pyrenean Mountain Dog where a double pair of hind-leg dew claws is a speciality of this breed.

The whole puppy should be lively and interested in life. There should be very little itching and scratching either in the pup of your choice or his fellows in the litter. An eight-week-old puppy does not have a very elegant walk but lameness for any reason is unacceptable.

At the end of this inspection you might be totally confident that all is well, that you were quite right in your choice of pup and that the cold-blooded assessment of his qualities has confirmed his selection. On the other hand, you might not feel so confident of your ability to 'vet' your potential purchase. In either instance, have the puppy examined by a vet of your choice. Good, reputable dog breeders never object to such a check up. Those who are trying to 'sell a pup' will dream up a dozen reasons why there is no need for a vet's advice. They might, for instance, claim to be frightened of the risk of infection being caught if the puppy is taken to the surgery. Rubbish; the same breeders take their dogs to dog shows where the dangers are no less. You may be told that their own vet has seen the puppies and said that they were all right. What probably happened is that he passed by the pen and, as a conversational gambit, remarked, 'That's a nice litter.' Vicars comment, 'What a lovely baby,' but that is not a guarantee of everlasting virtue.

If you have any doubts, or if you are less than certain about your own judgement, INSIST and have an examination by your vet before clinching the purchase. You're buying for a long time ahead; even with a perfect puppy there will be some troubles in the future, but if you start with a less than perfect one you will have no one but yourself to blame if more than the usual number of problems crop up.

A veterinary examination before purchase will cost between £5 and £10 at the Surgery and at least twice this if your vet has to visit the kennels to see the pup. This is very little when you think about the surveyor's charges when he came to look at the house that you were thinking about, and never bought.

After all this, we have arrived at a particular pup, so all that's left is to pay and take him home. Not quite. You have to hand over the money – a transaction that is rarely forgotten – but as well as the pup the vendor has to supply some paperwork. The price of a pedigree dog includes all the documents and signatures that are needed to register him at the Kennel Club. Without all this he is, from the breeding aspect, illegitimate. Perhaps the puppy has been given some type of vaccination against parvovirus, distemper or both while still with mother. If this is so, ask for a certificate of these injections so that when the time comes for his full vaccination your own vet knows exactly what has been given and when.

Puppy should have been wormed between four and five weeks of age. Check that this has been done, and if possible find out what wormer was used. Write down the name otherwise you will forget, which could make you feel inadequate if your vet asks you, 'Was he wormed before you got him, and what with?'

Stand firm and don't leave with puppy until you have all these details. The majority of dog breeders are honest and well organised so there is not a problem, but I have known difficulties when someone wants to register a pup only to find the breeder has moved, doesn't reply to letters or flatly refuses to sign a pedigree or transfer form claiming that the pup was sold at a 'pet' price which did not include his pedigree. A polite term for such behaviour is sharp practice. It's rare but it does happen. A practical way of dealing with the promise, 'I'll send on the papers,' is to reply, 'Thank you. I'll send on the cheque.'

Most breeders will supply a diet chart, which can be a very helpful and useful document but it is not a canine version of the ten commandments. Vets in practice see some extraordinary diet sheets making suggestions which no puppy would ever accept. I have treated a Yorkie pup for starvation because the diet sheet included an ounce of parsley each day for breakfast and an instruction not to give more food if the last meal had not been eaten. I do not believe that this dog breeder insisted that her own pups lived on parsley and I cannot explain why she should suggest it for any pup that she sold, but she did, and the pup nearly died.

Certainly find out what food your puppy has been weaned on to. Continue the same food for the first few days. If it is an unusual brand of biscuit meal or canned food collect some to take home with you so that pup can change homes without changing his diet. Far-sighted owners enquire about diets at least a week before collecting their pup so that the shopping is done and there is dog food in the larder before puppy arrives at his new home. There is no need to keep to the diet that he had in kennels. It may be much more convenient to feed a ready-prepared dog food from a can rather than cook some magic stew. But this change should be a gradual one and take ten days or so to complete.

The very best breeders – the most caring ones – will supply information about training your puppy. Unfortunately this 'after sales service' is seldom offered, so to any breeder who is reading this, why not start to offer training advice? Well-trained dogs are loved by everyone. Give your puppies the best possible start in their new life.

6 · Nursery school

From the first minute in his new home puppy starts to learn a new behaviour pattern. He has come to a strange place and he'll have to adjust to it. How he adjusts, is up to you.

Start as you mean to go on. It's no use putting off a disagreement with any new dog. You will win the mental battles while he's unsure of himself. When everything is new, he's willing (well, less unwilling) to accept that in this house dogs behave in certain ways – and humans decide what these ways are.

Dogs are pack animals and when puppy comes to live with you he is joining a new pack and within this pack there is a social order. He has to find his position. Make it crystal clear that he is lower in the pack than any human being. It matters little if the cat, the canary and the goldfish are lower down the order but all the family must be pack bosses. This is not unfair to the dog. He will not be cowed and subdued because he is a low caste. Rather he will be stress-free, knowing that there is always someone to protect him, to instruct him and to make decisions for him. The uncontrolled dog becomes confused: one minute he can do as he likes, the next minute he is told off or physically chastised for doing the same thing. That causes stress which in turn invites aggression. The dog fights to climb in the pack, he growls and snarls, perhaps bites, to establish himself. The canine rat race is an uncomfortable as any other.

If a puppy has to be admonished the best way is as the bitch would do to one of her recalcitrant youngsters. She would take him by the scruff of the neck and shake him. This works. It cuts a dominant, bossy pup down to size, but use such punishment very sparingly and rather gently. There is a danger of breaking a puppy's spirit (metaphorically) and destroying his confidence for all time.

Choose pup's sleeping room – and stick to this decision. He will be lonely, he will find it strange to be by himself in the dark, but don't weaken, don't have him up into your bedroom 'just this once'. It will become twice and before long it will be forever. The lessons learnt during the first ten weeks in his new home are all important and make the difference between a delightful-to-know dog that enjoys his life and gives pleasure to everyone he meets, and a self-opinionated unpleasant canine, a nuisance to his owner and not much pleasure to himself because no-one ever tells him that he's a wonderful dog. Approbation matters to every dog.

The journey home is lesson one. Unless puppy is one of the giant breeds take a cardboard box and some newspaper with you. Let him make the journey away from kennels, sitting in the box, with newspaper for bedding on the back seat of the car. If pup is a giant breed he may have to sit on the seat, on a blanket with paper as an extra protection. Any pup may be sick during his first car journey. If so, it's unfortunate but the box and paper will protect the car. The object of the lesson is simply to establish that good dogs sit quietly on the back seat of a car and when they do, their owner is very pleased.

Whilst on the subject of car travel, it is worthwhile investing in a little extra petrol and taking pup for a few minutes car ride once or twice a day during the first weeks at home. He may not be able to go outdoors for walks until all his vaccinations are complete but he can learn good car behaviour, and if he has thirty car rides before twelve weeks of age, he will never be car sick or worried about getting into a car.

We've reached home. You'll have to carry him indoors and all carrying is easier and safer if pup wears a collar at all times from the very beginning. A simple leather collar is best, fitting as snuggly as a man's collar when he's wearing a tie. Loose collars are dangerous because the dog can slip out of them and collars have been known to get caught on a projection – like a car door handle – and the dog hangs himself. There are two reasons for a collar from the very beginning. Firstly it should carry your name and address or phone number so that if the puppy does go walk-about a Good Samaritan can phone you to collect him, and secondly it allows you to control this lively youngster by slipping a finger beneath the collar whenever he is picked up. A surprising number of young dogs fall out of their owners' arms by wriggling forwards and if a small terrier pup drops that far it is equivalent to a child falling from the bedroom window. Small and toy breeds can, and often do, break a front leg by landing on it from this comparatively great height.

Once the pair of you are safely indoors, and the front door is closed, let puppy explore 'his' part of the house. And 'his' part is whatever rooms *you* have decided to share with him.

After a few minutes' survey it is time for some food, which introduces the feeding routine. What type of food is a separate question, covered in Ch 9. Make puppy sit a foot away from the dish. The collar helps this manœuvre; one hand in the collar, the other pushing his hindquarters to the ground, with a clearly spoken 'Sit' at the same time. Hold him in this position and make him wait for ten or twenty seconds (which must seem eternity to a hungry pup) and then just before his control breaks tell him 'All right' and he can jump up and eat.

If every meal follows this pattern, puppy will be sitting on command within only a week or so, and because he has discovered that obedience brings a tangible reward, this one command at least is firmly imprinted in his mind. He has also accepted that you are the provider, and he's beginning to accept that you are pack leader and give the instructions. If training progresses no further than obedience to 'Sit', life is safer for the dog and easier for the owner than a life without any obedience. Whenever something is going wrong 'Sit' allows you to catch up with things. Either to put a lead on, to stop the dog rushing into the road, chasing the cat or setting off with the intention of seducing that beautiful bitch.

One dog breeder who teaches her puppies this lesson from six weeks of age sold a pup of nine weeks. Twenty-four hours later the new owner phoned to say that the pup would not eat. As soon as any food was put down, he sat by the dish, looked hungry and was actually salivating, but would not eat. The breeder had omitted to tell the new owner that these pups expected to sit, and then expected to be told to eat. I won't award the puppy high marks for intelligence, but 100% for rapid learning and obedience.

Once the sitting and waiting routine is established, walking on a lead can be taught by exploiting a love of food. Put the food down as normal, but make puppy sit at the opposite side of the room, as far away from his dish as possible. Then, with his lead attached to the collar, tell him it is all right to eat. He will walk on the lead in front of you, eager to get to the dish, thus learning that leads are nothing to get uptight about. So often a pup behaves like a fish on the end of a line when he first experiences a lead and everyone has seen unthinking owners trying to teach a dog to accept a lead by dragging him along behind them.

Back to day one. Once the first feed is over take puppy outside to the most secluded corner of the garden (I hope it is a dry day). There is a very good chance that the excitement of arrival and the stimulus of food will make something happen, be it urine or motion. Stay outdoors in this area until it does, and when it does, congratulate your dog. Make it very clear that you are pleased and so he begins to learn that this part of the garden is his lavatory. Teaching him the correct place is much more effective than any telling off when a puddle or mess is found in the house. Saying 'No' is negative training, and unless the 'No' is synchronous with a misdemeanour, it is ineffective because a dog's mind cannot associate a telling off with his actions some minutes or hours earlier.

And so to bed. Puppies' lives consist of short periods of hectic activity and then a couple of hours of deep sleep when exhaustion sets in. He's ready for a snooze by now. You have decided where he will sleep – the kitchen or breakfast room are the commonest choices. I'm not enthusiastic about a dog having the run of the house, and certainly not a puppy. I'm even less enthusiastic about the dog sleeping in the bedroom – or on the bed. But it's your dog and your bed.

Assuming commonsense prevails, the cardboard box that he came home in makes an excellent sleeping box. Place the box on its side, open end towards the wall. Several layers of newspaper provide all the bedding needed. Pup now has a private cave with a roof over his head, and no one can see him because the entrance is concealed. It is quite dark inside this den, which is conducive to sleep, and newspaper is warm and dry. If the box is just big enough he feels tightly enclosed by the cardboard walls and this creates an atmosphere of security.

An alternative, albeit an unsatisfactory one, is a new wicker basket (one that is big enough for him when he grows up), and a lovely soft cushion to lie on. The poor pup perches on top of the cushion like a cockerel on top of a haystack, and he is totally exposed to view from every direction as well as any cold draughts that happen to be wafting around. The edges of the basket appear miles away. He's all alone in a great big world. I'm not a dog and I can't think dog thoughts but I do believe that puppy in his cardboard box is likely to think he's safer, feel cosier and so sleep better.

There are many 'tips' for comforting a puppy and encouraging a whole night's sleep. A hot water bottle is said to simulate the warmth that mother and his litter mates provided. It is suggested that the tick of a clock sounds like another dog's heart beat and convinces him that he is not alone. Perhaps such comforters work, given adequate faith. I do not have it. Of course a cold puppy is likely to be miserable – and tell you so – but a warm room, protection from draughts, and insulated bedding last all through the night, whereas everyone knows what a hot-water bottle feels like at dawn on a cold morning. Closed curtains stop dawn sunshine causing an extra-early wake-up and provide some sound-proofing so that outside noise is not a disturbance.

A full stomach is the best soporific and every animal is inclined to sleep after feeding. Cows lie down to chew their cud. Lions in the Zoo are at their least interesting half an hour after feeding time – they are fast asleep. A snake swallows something larger than its own diameter and sleeps for days. Puppies are no exception, so make the largest meal of the day the last one before bedtime.

A full bladder disturbs sleep, so before bedtime another trip to the bottom of the garden – staying there until something happens – helps to prevent noises in the night. And don't forget the congratulations when 'it' happens.

There is no reason why any puppy should not be nearly dry and clean at night from the very start. I say nearly, because there are bound to be odd mishaps. The most effective toilet training consists of telling the puppy what to do, and where, so if there is anything to clean up on the morning after, don't ever punish or even be cross with the puppy. He does not, cannot, make any connection between leaving his box and urinating at 3 am and being shouted at at 7 am. He may learn that the sight of a motion on the floor is very unpopular with his owner, and in extreme cases puppy tries to hide the evidence by eating his own motion because his pack leader does not like to see it, but he is then told off for trying to please. Training by saying 'No' often produces a very confused dog that could not be blamed for thinking that there is little justice in this world.

Breeders of toy dogs sometimes train puppies to use newspapers scattered over the floor as their toilet area and suggest that a new puppy should continue such a routine in his new home 'until he is old enough to go outside'. This only suggests that their pups are so frail and delicate that a breath of fresh air will be fatal, and if you believe this danger, don't contemplate buying such a weakling. I am totally opposed to the newspaper routine. It encourages the pup to soil his living area – your house. When the time arrives to allow access to the great outdoors this pup has to unlearn his existing habits and start to learn to use that patch at the bottom of the garden. What was right is now wrong. More confusion. Similarly I would advise against scattering newspapers around the floor 'just in case'. This is an invitation, tantamount to erecting signs reading 'Ladies' or 'Gents'. If the floor covering is not washable and has to be protected, thick polythene sheeting over the whole area causes less confusion in the pup's mind.

Puppies have a natural instinct to follow their mother until they are about fifteen weeks of age. When they have left Mum, the instinct remains and they follow their owner. Thus, training a dog to come when called is easier if the lessons start when the instinct points in the desired direction. Short lessons, about five minutes long twice a day, always using the same phrase to tell him to come to you, are most effective. When he comes to the call, always congratulate him, and a tit-bit now and again reinforces your approval. There are advantages in using one of the high-pitched dog whistles. It is distinctive and when he's grown up and has to be called in a park or similar public place it may be less embarrassing, and more effective to use a whistle than a raucous or shrill shriek. If he does not respond to a call or whistle, walk away from him, there's a very good chance that he will follow and so obey, even if a little late. Make all training half lesson, half play, and several short-duration lessons are more effective than longer ones. Puppies soon become bored and they cannot concentrate for many minutes at a time.

To discourage puppy growing up into a possessive dog that snarls at anyone who goes near his food dish and will bite his owner rather than give up a bone or favourite toy, take things away from him at a very early stage. From time to time take his food away, while he's feeding. This teaches him that you, his pack leader, can take food away, and he also learns that the food will come back again when you decide – which won't be very long. He won't go hungry.

At some time in his later life puppy will need grooming; a bone may become stuck in his mouth; his nails might need attention, and there is a high possibility that his feet will have to be wiped clean. Without early training, many dog owners are quite unable to give their dog any of these attentions.

If a puppy learns to accept a comb, around his feet and ears as well as along his back, he is more likely to be well groomed because every combing need not start with a fight with the dog. Arrange a two-minute lesson every day. Place the pup on a smooth-topped table and go through a routine of combing, opening his mouth, looking down his ears, picking up his feet and lifting his tail (dogs sometimes need attention at that end). This education means that the dog grows up to accept this type of handling as part of everyday life and if he has to be given ear drops or eye drops years later the early training will be remembered and less angst and more effective treatment will ensue. If puppy is brought up to have his mouth opened from time to time he will suffer much less if a bone becomes stuck across the roof of his mouth because his owner will be able to remove it without a great fight and struggle. Many dogs endure more than they need simply because their owner is unable to administer simple treatments. That's almost as great a neglect as not feeding the dog.

Lessons learnt before four months of age determine a dog's behaviour for the rest of his life. If he learns to accept his place within the family he is certain to have a very comfortable and stress-free life. Everyone will approve of this dog, and there is a touch of the Uriah Heep in every canine. They are ever so 'umble, and wallow in praise and approbation. Some of this glory reflects on the owner – and you feel two inches taller when your paragon takes you for a walk.

For your dog's sake, for your sake and for the sake of those few dog haters, find time (make time) to produce a well mannered dog. If all dogs were as pleasant as the best 10%, even the anti-dog brigade would find reasons for enjoying dog company.

7 · Second-hand dogs

In the last chapter I talked at great length about training a puppy to behave in an acceptable way. But everyone does not start with a pup. Second-hand dogs are re-homed and they may need training as well.

In many ways the adult dog is a more difficult pupil. Young puppies have no fixed ideas, and possess an open, receptive mind. A two-year-old dog has learnt behaviour patterns. He might not be 'trained' in any conventional sense, but he does know what he can get away with and he might have had to learn to survive by being aggressive. He has to unlearn bad habits and re-learn acceptable ones.

The same basic principles apply whatever the age but an adult dog is bigger so problems are compounded if any physical conflict develops between pet and owner. However, it is amazing how many dogs respond to positive, clear instructions. This is how most of the 'instant' dog trainers work. They take a dog that has never been given a positive instruction that he could understand in his life. By voice and some physical pressure the dog is told what to do by a complete stranger. A totally new experience for the dog, so, because he is not sure of what is going on, his response is to obey and do as this potential pack leader indicates.

Every vet in practice sees this scenario when mother and two uncontrolled children arrive with a dog spinning at the end of a lead. The dog is seen quite quickly, perhaps before his turn, because the children are disorganising all the nice piles of reading matter and 'please take one' leaflets in the waiting room. In the consulting room the dog continues to move in every possible way except walking quietly at heel and the children prepare to extend their destruction zone to anything moveable or breakable at unruly child height. If the dog is placed on the examination table and told, in a fairly firm voice, to sit and behave himself, he looks surprised and remains still, awaiting the next instruction. A bellow in the direction of the children with instructions to stand quietly on either side of mother and touch nothing is usually equally effective. Well-behaved children, strangely enough, always arrive with a well-behaved dog. There must be a moral here.

Training adult dogs does not require partial strangulation with a metal choke collar. This should not need saying, but one does see dogs almost pulled off their feet by owners who will not accept this view.

Dogs for new homes fall into two groups: those that come directly from one home to a new one; and the true strays from a Rescue Home. Taking on a known dog can have many advantages. The middle-aged pet of a very old lady, now deceased, may be an excellent companion for someone getting on in years. This dog has developed a leisurely, somewhat slow-moving life style, ready-made for a retirement home. Next door's dog that enjoyed playing with the children may fit perfectly into your young family if next door emigrate and can't take their pet. But the old lady's dog might be panic stricken and unhappy if placed with children who have not been part of his life during the past seven years. And the children-enjoying dog may develop destructive habits when he finds an elderly household very boring. It's just the same as keeping any other pet; the right pet in the right place means success, anything else means varying degrees of disaster.

The dog with no known background from a Home can be a problem and I would never advise a first-time dog owner to start in this way.

I know it is not the dog's fault. He can be re-trained. But the dog lover with time and experience to re-programme a mixed-up orphan, already has a dog or dogs and neither time, space nor money to take on more. Many first-time owners fail and are put off for ever. I get at least two letters every week saying something like, 'Bonzo was a year old when I got him from ... Dogs Home. Now he won't stay in ... isn't clean at nights ... growls at the children ... bites the postman ... or some other misdemeanour. Do you think he will grow out of it?' Poor dog hasn't got a chance. He's almost certain to have been punished when he returned from his wanderings, had his nose rubbed in his own faeces and been chosen as a guard dog and then blamed when he bites anyone other than a modern Bill Sykes. No dog living could benefit from or understand such 'training'.

There is no such thing as a lost dog. Only unfound ones, and these are not found because nobody ever looked for them. If a well-loved dog goes astray his owner haunts the police station, the RSPCA Office, local veterinary surgeries, and advertises, offering a reward. There is a very good chance of finding that dog, and if the dog had only been wearing a collar plus name and address, the finding would have happened earlier. But if an undisciplined, uncared-for, latch-key dog fails to return home, the feckless owner of this dog doesn't bother. He can get a new puppy, and no-one was very fond of that dog anyhow.

This untrained dog becomes the 'stray', kept for seven days and then destroyed unless he finds a home. This is the dog that first-time dog owners cannot cope with, because they do not have the ability, time or enthusiasm to re-train him.

If, in spite of all the above, you do 'give one a good home' be prepared to spend time and effort for several months, before he becomes a dog that you are proud to own. Perseverance pays. I hope your perseverance persists.

8 · What about a cat?

'I like them' is the best reason for choosing any animal, and if your choice is a cat, instead of, or as well as a dog, the best starting point is a kitten. Many a cossetted cat is said to live where he does solely because he turned up one cold, wet evening and stayed. The cat that came in from the cold makes a much better story than one that turned up on a bright summer morning but if statistics were kept I believe they would show that more strays walk in between May and September than the rest of the year. Cats have more sense than to wander when it's wet and miserable outdoors.

If you are deciding to take on a cat, rather than be taken over by one, a kitten is the best starting point and spring-time is kitten time.

More than 50% of dogs are pedigree and the variations in size and shape are enormous. Less than 5% of cats are pedigree and whatever the lineage, cats' sizes vary little. A weight range of nine to fourteen pounds includes the vast majority of adult cats. Temperament varies a little with the breeds – Siamese tend to be vocal. Hair length varies, but non-pedigrees can have as thick and long a coat as any other cat.

A cat is for ever, so spend time choosing. Decide on the breed that you want. Never, never underestimate the time (and devotion) that is involved in keeping a long-haired cat groomed so that he looks and feels respectable. If you think that a good combing now and again is enough, believe me, it isn't.

Decide which sex of cat you prefer. Perhaps you have decided that whatever the sex, it will be neutered. Remember there is a difference in temperament between neutered males (bold, brash and big) and speyed females (more fastidious, gentler, somewhat smaller).

If you have any thought of breeding kittens, your choice must be a female kitten as a household cat. It may sound an attractive proposition to keep a pedigree tom cat, and perhaps even holiday on the proceeds of his labours (he is an essential ingredient in the production of pedigree kittens), but, pedigree or not, an un-neutered tom cat does not make a good house pet. They are delightful characters but when Spring comes around every tom worthy of the name sets off on his travels with one idea in his mind – and when he achieves his ambition he does not wait to collect any stud fee to pay you for his keep throughout the rest of the year. Pedigree-stud toms must be confined during the breeding season at least. And every entire male

Temperament varies a little between different cat breeds. Never underestimate the time involved in grooming long-haired cats.

cat has the distinctive tom-cat smell which permeates any house that he lives in.

Once the breed, sex and perhaps colour is sorted out, the source is the next important decision. Always get a kitten from the home he was born into. Change of home at seven or eight weeks of age is a stressful experience for any kitten. If he goes to a pet shop, or Cat's Home, at seven weeks of age and then moves again to you at eight weeks, he has two changes of diet and environment which can cause stress and produce an upset, unwell kitten. Even if your choice is a pedigree cat look for a breeder near to your home, within easy driving distance at least. There is a strange (and incorrect) idea that any pedigree kitten from the other end of the country must be better than a locally bred one.

The best source of pet kittens is from a family house that includes children. Kittens born into this environment are handled from a very early age and grow up at ease with people and enjoy being picked up.

Early training is very important in determining a kitten's behaviour, and inherited temperament is of much less significance. A cat's attitude to life seems to depend solely on its experiences between three and eight weeks of age. The cat from the house full of children relaxes when he is picked up. He'll lie in anyone's arms, claws sheathed, content and convinced that his place is with people. A kitten that is born on a farm, in a warehouse or away from people in any manner, and is not handled or stroked until he is ready to leave his mother, does not learn to relax, is never at ease on anyone's lap or in their arms. He's a spikey cat with claws half out and muscles tense whenever humans are about. He's suspicious of people.

Try to find the kitten that is to be yours when he is two or three weeks old – and there is no harm in choosing, provisionally at least, before a kitten is born. If mother cat is the breed and colour that you are looking for, then a 'keep for me' label on an unborn kitten is quite appropriate.

Seven to eight weeks is the right age to change homes. This is young enough to allow a kitten to learn to socialise with humans. Some breeders of pedigree cats insist that nine to twelve weeks is better. The kitten is older and less stressful, they argue. True, as far as physical upset is concerned, but a twelve-week-old kitten that has stayed with Mum and his litter-mates has begun to socialise with cats – not humans. If one pet cat is going to enjoy living with you – and you with him – the cat should become accustomed to this lifestyle at an early age. Most of the physical stress can be avoided if kittens are introduced to solid food from four weeks of age, so that leaving mother and moving to a diet of cat food at seven weeks is not so great and sudden a change. This early introduction to solid food takes much of the strain off a nursing-mother cat especially if she is trying to feed a litter of five or six.

Although you might have reserved a kitten before he was born there comes a day when you have to make the positive decision that *this* kitten is to be *the* one. Look very closely and choose with a cold heart. You want to start with a healthy kitten, physically perfect. Here is a check list:

Nose: this should be clean, even shaped, both nostrils the same size, no discharge, no sneezing.

Teeth: should meet evenly; at this age they will be baby teeth and every tooth that you see now will be lost and replaced by the time the kitten is six months old. But they should be correctly aligned now.

Eyes: look for clean, bright eyes that are wide open. There should not be any excess tears or discharge. Do not believe it if you are told that 'it's the sawdust', or 'just a bit of a cold in the eye, cold tea will cure it'. Messy eyes could be the prelude to all sorts of troubles. Start with perfect ones.

Ears: again should be clean. A dark brown wax in them may indicate ear-mite infection. Easy to clear up, but the breeder of the cat should have seen to this, not started you off with a kitten with ear trouble. Lice, which should never be there, can be found around the ears. Kittens should not shake their heads – this is another sign of ear mites.

Legs: no lameness. A kitten of seven weeks of age is not a very elegant mover but he should scamper about, not hold one paw up in the air when-

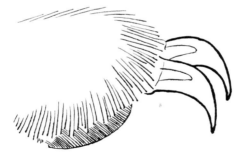

Double claws — where there should only be one

ever he stands still. Count the toes. There should be four on each foot, with a dew claw on the inside of the front legs. Some cats have extra toes. This disqualifies them from shows and the nails on supernumerary toes can overgrow and cause troubles throughout a cat's life.

Coat: this should be clean, free from lice, fleas or specks of black grit – which is probably flea dirt. Healthy kittens do not have to carry fleas, and cat keeping does not mean that flea keeping is inevitable. There should not be any hairless patches either.

The rear end: it is not indelicate to inspect this part of a kitten. Look under the tail. There should be no signs of diarrhoea nor any redness or soreness. Check the sex of the kitten at this end. 'She had such a pretty face,' is not a reliable method of sexing. Every vet in practice expects that there will be at least a 10% error in the sexes of the kitten brought for neutering or innoculations. Henry is re-christened Henrietta and Tabitha becomes Tom. Misdiagnoses are in either direction. Experienced breeders can be relied upon to sort out the sexes for you, but if you are in doubt distance is the guide. The distance between the anus and the next visible opening is greatest in the male.

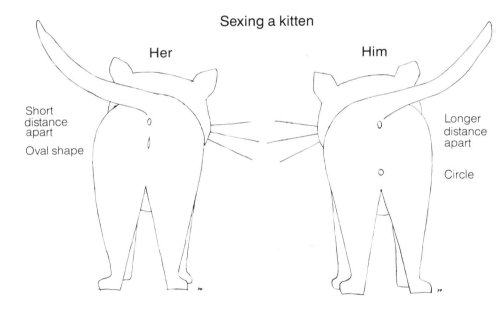

Sexing a kitten

Her   Him

Short distance apart

Oval shape

Longer distance apart

Circle

Mother, and the rest of the litter: all cats on the premises should appear healthy. If there are sneezes, sore eyes, or signs of diarrhoea in other cats, the kitten that you choose could be the next to succumb.

There is one other check that should be made if possible, although seven or eight weeks old might be too soon. Be certain that a tom kitten has both testicles descended and in the scrotum. This development fails in a few cats. If one testicle only is descended the animal is described as a monorchid; if both fail to descend this is a cryptorchid. In neither instance can the cat be shown. A monorchid can breed, although it is unwise to allow this in pedigree cats because the condition may be inherited. A cryptorchid is infertile, because a retained testicle, in the abdomen, is at too high a temperature to allow normal sperm to develop. Normal sex hormones are produced by crytorchid cats so they wander and smell just as any fully fertile tom. Castration is quite possible, and essential if they are to live as part of the family, but it is a much more complex and expensive operation in the imperfectly developed male.

After all those check points you might feel like someone who has just read a medical encyclopaedia, and is suffering from mental indigestion. If you are doubtful of your own ability to 'vet' your new kitten it is not unreasonable to ask your vet to examine him before you actually complete the purchase, or accept the gift. Remember the proverb about looking gift horses in the mouth! The odd, old fashioned breeder might resent this check on his stock. Good breeders welcome it because they are confident that nothing wrong will be found. The cost of such an examination at the vet's surgery will be between £5 and £10 in most cases.

You've decided on *the* kitten and you want to hurry home with it. Whoa, slow down again. Find out if it has been wormed (all kittens should be wormed between four and six weeks of age). If you're paying for a pedigree kitten, a part of the cost is that piece of paper. Don't be put off with, 'I'll send it on.' Sometimes people remember to bank your cheque but forget to post the pedigree. Find out which food the kitten has been weaned on to.

It is possible that some vaccinations have been done already. The usual age for these injections is twelve weeks but some catteries do immunise kittens from six weeks of age. If your kitten has had such injections make certain that you collect the certificate so that when the twelve-week injections are due you are able to tell your vet precisely what has been given beforehand. Perhaps you will be told that the kitten is from Feline Leukaemia-tested parents and wonder what this means. There is a leukaemia that affects cats and is caused by a virus. Blood testing can indicate if a cat colony is infected or not and some pedigree breeders test for this. It is not a guarantee that your kitten could never become infected but it does indicate that the human parents of your new kitten are taking every care possible.

Now it is time to leave with the kitten. You have bought a cat carrier I trust. The good ones are costly but it is worthwhile and as this kitten is going to be with you for at least fourteen years, £20 plus for the basket is not too much. I prefer the plastic or plastic-coated metal-mesh carrying cages to wicker ones for three reasons. Most cats like to know where they are going and travel contentedly if they can see out. Plastic, or metal covered in plastic, is easy to clean. Anyone who has tried to clean a wicker basket after a diarrhoeic cat has had an accident knows the difficulties presented by a woven floor. Many wicker baskets have an ill-fitting door, held by leather strap hinges, and an able-bodied cat finds little difficulty in escaping.

Avoid the temptation to fill the basket with soft bedding and blankets. Paper, possibly newspaper, is the best covering for the carrier floor. It's clean, sterile from a cat disease aspect, easy to obtain and easy to dispose of by burning. Blankets, sheets and cushions need washing – and don't always get it – and they can occupy a lot of space. I've seen many a cat basket so full of soft cushions that there is barely room for the cat and he must come out with a very stiff neck because he had to travel in a head-down, praying position once the lid was closed upon him. There is one newspaper disadvantage with white or very light-coloured cats: the print can come off and make the cat look very grubby, so unprinted paper is best for these colours. I don't believe that the printer's ink is in any way harmful to cats in the quantities that can come off a printed sheet, just messy.

Home at last and his first introduction to a new world. A properly brought up kitten is curious, confident and eager to find out. Let him. If there are other pets already in residence the new kitten should meet them as soon as possible. There will be hisses and spits, but noises don't hurt. The key to a successful introduction is to leave it to the animals, but be there to interfere in a serious crisis, and most important of all, arrange it so that either animal can make an honourable retreat. Real fights, real injuries, occur when your old cat or dog has to defend his territory against this new interloper. If he could have sidled out through the door, gone to rest behind the settee, or if the new kitten had somewhere to hide so that eyeball-to-eyeball conflict was avoided, then so would fights.

Cardboard boxes are useful places of retreat and make a very good kitten bed. Place the box on its side, with the opening towards the wall. Newspaper makes the best box lining. Kitten can go into the box – and he will – where there is a roof over his head and he's facing the wall so that there is a high degree of privacy. The new kitten can hide and feel safe. The old cat does not have to notice and can pretend that the kitten does not exist. Honour is satisfied. Amicable relationships almost always develop between new and old pets, but it might take three months before all is sweetness and light.

As soon as the kitten realises that this new household provides food he has a very strong reason for settling down. A kitten of eight weeks old needs four meals a day. Make the last meal at night the largest one – a full tummy is conducive to sleep.

Whatever goes in must come out, which introduces the subject of toilet training. Cats always intend to be clean – by their standards. Training means directing natural instincts of cleanliness so that cat behaviour coin-

(*Top*) Cardboard boxes are useful places of retreat. (*Above*) Grooming is easiest on a smooth surface where the cat cannot get a grip. (*Right*) The same applies when administering pills.

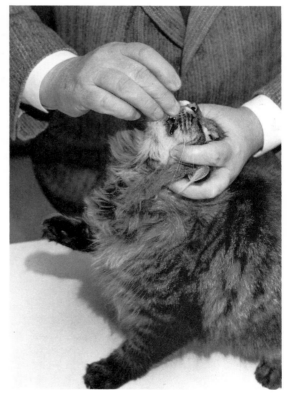

cides with our human ideas. How you train depends to an extent on what you wish to achieve and how your house is organised. One thing is certain, training by punishment or telling off after an accident is totally ineffective. Teach the cat what *to do* rather than what *not* to do.

If you want to train him to use the great outdoors, then I suggest that you start, even at eight weeks, to indicate that outside is the right place. This might mean keeping a litter tray just outside the back door. If the weather is wet, keep the tray in a waterproof box – an old tea chest on its side or something like an old-fashioned dog kennel. This will keep the litter dry and gives the kitten a degree of privacy and security. The great outdoors must be little frightening for a tiny kitten. He feels very vulnerable while he's digging a hole and concentrating, so dry litter to dig in attracts him, and surrounding walls and a roof over his head mean that he does not have to worry about an enemy cat attacking while he's defenceless.

If he is to use a tray indoors the same routine of pointing in the right direction applies. Frequently renewed litter encourages the kitten; a smelly tray is as repulsive to them as it is to us. Almost every kitten should be totally clean by twelve weeks of age and many are without mistake from the very first day – if the owner is co-operative in providing the facilities.

When your kitten first joins you he has to learn many things – he will learn how to behave and how to react whether you teach him or not. He might learn to resent being combed, and learn that if he struggles, you stop combing him, so he has won that battle of wills. He might learn that if he looks hungrily at the fridge you will weaken and a small piece of the Sunday joint is provided. Very much better for all if he learns that you are in charge and you make the deicsions. Early lessons are the most effective.

Handling is easiest if the cat is placed on a table which has a smooth surface. The cat cannot get a grip to help his struggles and the human is working at a convenient and natural height. So one early lesson is to comb him. An eight-week-old short-haired kitten hardly needs to see a comb, but he should learn that combing happens. It's not very unpleasant, and the sooner he behaves well, the sooner he can go about his own affairs again. While he is on the table look into his ears, and his eyes. Open his mouth, look under his tail, lie him on his back and look at his tummy. Part game, part training, but these early lessons can save trouble later on when, or if, he develops ear trouble at three years old, and you have to put drops in his ears. The trained kitten is likely to be better treated, the drops reach the right place more easily, and the ears recover quickly. The untrained, uncontrolled cat may remain untreated because the owner finds administration of drops, pills or eye ointment too difficult.

If your kitten is long haired and light coloured, an introduction to bathing is worthwhile before too much time has passed. Washing him, and making him fit to be seen (or shown) may occupy a significant amount of time in the future. The sooner the pair of you reach agreement as to who is to win the battles of the bath, the better. Hair driers help afterwards, and a kitten should also learn that the buzzing noise is totally harmless and grown-up cats don't panic.

At bedtime, many owners spend hours calling their cat. Because cats are semi-nocturnal animals he may think that dusk is hunting time and so has no wish to hear the call. If he hears a noise that might be to his advantage, a return home is more likely. The noise of a can opener can be effective but if a kitten is brought up to hear a high-pitched dog whistle as his full food dish is placed on the floor, he will come running when the whistle blast says 'Grub's up.'

Just as a healthy child searches around until he (or she – original sin is not wholly a male attribute) finds something to do wrong, so will a kitten find something that annoys. One of the best ways of telling him 'No' is a wetting from a water pistol. If a cat discovers that every time he jumps on the kitchen table, or sharpens his claws on the three-piece, he gets a wetting, he will begin to associate his action with this unpleasant experience. He does not blame his owner, and there is no danger of causing any damage to the cat by a jet of clean water. Smacking may cause unreasonable pain, and the aim is to train the cat, not injure him. When my two kittens, Bacon and Egg, were small, they were so into people and so self-confident that they believed that their place was on our laps as soon as we sat down for any meal. After three weeks with a water pistol as part of the table setting their behaviour at meal times had improved considerably.

9 · Feeding dogs and cats

Supplying enough of the correct type of food at properly spaced intervals, is a basic responsibility for any owner of any animal. This does not mean that feeding has to be complicated and the best foods need not be those that take the most trouble to prepare. Dogs and cats are carnivores, so their diet must be based on meat. Dogs survive, and sometimes thrive, on strange diets containing only a minimum quantity of animal protein, which does not prove that such diets are satisfactory, only that adult dogs are very adaptable. Cats are more precise in their requirements because, unlike dogs, their bodies cannot make certain vitamins and proteins, even when the necessary basic substances are present in the food. Some things have to come ready made for a cat.

All pet owners want to do the very best for their pet and many believe that because meat is the natural food, the best quality that money can buy is essential. Another belief is that any dog or cat knows what is good for it and the most reliable guide to proper feeding is the animal's own taste. With all respect to these very concerned and caring people, this is utter nonsense, and pandering blindly to any animal's likes and dislikes is the most effective way of creating some deficiency in the diet.

It is perfectly true that the wild ancestors of today's pets caught their prey and ate it – sometimes. Wild dogs were scavengers. Anything animal, newly killed by them or long dead and putrefying, made a meal, while beetles or maggots added flavour. Horrible thought to us, but this liking for carrion might explain why well brought up dogs enjoy a roll on a rotting rabbit carcass. They are just going back in time to ancestral tastes. But wild dogs would never have eaten meat alone. Their meal was a bit of flesh, a bit of bone, some skin and offal, and fur or feathers provided fibre. This mixture of the whole carcase supplied protein and fat from the flesh, calcium and phosphorous from bone, vitamin A and D from the liver, vitamin B from liver and bowel, while the indigestible solids gave useful bulk. Although most cats shun carrion they too would eat most parts of their freshly killed prey in a wild existence. Some of this instinct persists after many generations of domestication in that cats prefer food at room temperature or even a little warmer. Straight from the fridge is not the way to a cat's heart.

Prepared foods made specifically for dogs and cats are undoubtedly the simplest and easiest way of giving a properly balanced diet to any pet. There are two provisos. Buy a reputable make. There are bags and cans without any manufacturer's name. Avoid these and choose a brand that the maker is prepared to own. Secondly, read the instructions. A lot of care goes into the preparation of pet food. It's wasted if the food is then wrongly fed.

There are three main types of food. Canned foods first. These contain around 75% moisture – the same amount as meat or offal. There are two types of canned dog foods. One, intended to be fed alone, contains meat and cereal. The other, more expensive sort, contains meat products only and is intended for mixing with biscuits. Because biscuits are cheaper than canned food the costs of feeding the dog vary little whichever can is involved. There are some 'special' foods for toy dogs, which contain rather more fat, hence more energy and this fat seems to add to flavour. They are very palatable.

Canned cat foods are formulated for feeding alone and all the major manufacturers make certain that those amino acids essential to cats are in their feeds. Cats have a limited ability to use cereals and so meat and cereal foods are not made for them. Semi-moist foods contain about 25% water – somewhat less than fresh bread, which is around 40%. Meat products are the major ingredient and most dogs find this type of food very acceptable. Cats vary, some find it very palatable, others can take it or leave it.

Dry foods – less than 10% water – include dog biscuits, or course, and a large variety of complete diets for dogs, and meals for mixing with canned food or natural meat products. Some dry foods are intended to have water added before use. This may make them much more acceptable. Many dogs are not enthusiastic about finely ground, dry feeds. While dogs in kennels may eat them with apparent enjoyment, because the threat of a kennel mate swallowing the lot is a great stimulant to appetite, the dog living without canine company and competition is often more fastidious.

Dry cat food can cause problems in certain cases. These compounded foods contain all the necessary nutrients, but very little fluid (7%–10% on average). This means that the cat has to obtain almost all his fluid by drinking and a few cats don't drink enough to make up for the water that is not in the food. Thus their urine becomes very concentrated and salts in the urine may crystallise out to form a sandy, gravelly-type material that is an intense irritant to the lining of the bladder. Cystitis is caused, which is painful in the female cat and life-endangering in the male because the tiny bladder stones can block the urethra and prevent him passing urine. Every packet of dried cat biscuits has a message printed on it about providing fresh milk or water at all times. The cat cannot read the instructions, and some owners do not, but they are important. Cats like the 'crunchiness' of dry food and the hard biscuits help to clean and polish the teeth. Dry food is not really suitable for young kittens though most adult cats thrive on it. But if a cat has ever suffered from any bladder trouble it is unwise to feed this type of food to that particular animal. Perhaps the best of both worlds is to feed canned food for most of the cat's needs and a few dry cat biscuits each day to clean and polish the teeth. My cats make do by stealing the dog's biscuits to use as their tooth brush and if the noise they make crunching them into powder is anything to go by, thoroughly enjoy the jaw exercise.

The very first dry cat foods were much more prone to cause bladder sand because they contained high levels of magnesium salts, the basic material from which crystals form. This has now been corrected and this part of the danger eliminated.

Meat (minced or not), tripe, chicken, and fish are all on sale for pet feeding. Such meats must be produced under conditions that would make them fit for human consumption if they are sold in an uncooked state, so there should be no worry about having such meats in the kitchen. However any raw meat is a possible source of nasty bugs that no one wants in their food so good hygiene and separate plates are sensible safety measures. Any of these meats, mixed with good quality biscuits make a suitable diet for an adult dog; cats and puppies may need extra minerals or vitamins. How much extra, poses a problem. Perhaps the best solution is to buy a good quality feed supplement and give the minimum quantity. Too much added calcium or any other trace element and excess vitamin dosage can be as harmful as any shortage. Getting the extras absolutely right needs an analytical laboratory at the bottom of the garden.

All this is leading up to my advice about feeding one or two family pets: give them prepared food and let someone else worry about the right mixture. Because canned foods are the most palatable I prefer this type, and, more importantly, so does the pet. The fondness of an animal for his owner may not be in direct proportion to the palatability of the food provided but the way to a pet's heart passes very close to his stomach. This does not mean that the pet decides. The few deficiency diseases that we see nowadays are almost always in the over-cared-for pet that is allowed to dictate his own menu. One example is the toy dog that won't eat anything but minced rump steak (his owner's words, not mine). Because this diet is almost totally deficient in calcium and phosphorus, the dog develops very fragile bones, which may fracture as a result of quite normal day to day mini-bumps.

I'll always remember one Papillon, the apple of her owner's eye, who was allowed the run of the house, nowhere was out of bounds. She fell off the bed and broke one front leg. We put the damaged bits together and fixed them with a stainless-steel pin. The reason for the fracture was quite obvious during the operation. This dog's radius (the major bone of the front leg) was little thicker than an eggshell – a typical 'all meat' dog. She went home, limping, and with very strict instructions about diet, including mineral and vitamin supplements. Three days later the dog was back again with the other front leg broken. She had been allowed on the bed again, and tripped over the eiderdown. She hadn't even fallen to the ground, but the bone was so fragile that a simple stumble on to a totally soft landing was more than the bone could tolerate. It was an extreme example of over indulgence actually causing suffering.

Cat owners who allow their cat to demand, and get, nothing except raw liver can cause intense pain to their pet. Not a deficiency in this instance but an excess of Vitamin A from the liver. Extra bony lumps develop in the vertebrae and cause a very painful and stiff neck. One of the early signs of this condition is the cat beginning to look very unkempt. It's just too painful to turn round and groom himself. If things are allowed to go on and the diet is not corrected, he finishes up almost unable to walk and in constant pain. There's no doubt this cat enjoyed the liver, but he paid a heavy price.

Those are just two examples, but they show that buying the 'best' and 'letting him choose' are not good ways of feeding pets. How much and how often? are questions that worry. Let's take puppies and kittens first.

Young things need more food, more often. Pups in particular grow at an enormous rate. A new-born terrier weighs about five ounces: when he has finished growing at a year old he should weight twenty-four pounds, which is around eighty times his birth weight in a year. I have weighed grey-hounds at eight weeks of age and they gain up to eight ounces per day. By comparison I am told that humans multiply their birth weight by three in the first year of life, and 8 ounces in a week would be almost unprecedented.

By three months of age pups need more food than they will when fully grown. A useful feeding frequency is:

4 meals per day up to 12 weeks old
3 meals per day from 3–5 months, and then
2 meals per day for the rest of the time, or drop to one meal after about 9 months old.

Always make the last meal of the day the largest one. The overnight interval is the longest gap and a full tummy is a soporific.

How much, is best answered by reading the instructions on the can or packet and following them intelligently. They are a guide, not one of the Ten Commandments. If, in spite of anything I have written, puppy is being reared on meat and biscuit meal, think in terms of half to three-quarters of a pound of meat per day for an eight-week-old Labrador, going up to a pound at three months, and at least one and a half pounds at four months, plus a similar weight of biscuits. These amounts are *per day* before anyone misreads my suggestions and gives them per meal.

Kitten growth is less explosive, but a four-ounce kitten at birth becomes a ten-pound cat at a year old. His meal times should be similar to a pup of the same age and quantity suggestions are on every can. How much, is partly judgement also, but a 400-gm can should last a ten-week-old kitten about three days. Each meal should be eaten within ten minutes. Don't leave uneaten food about; pups or kittens learn that it's always there and become miserable feeders. If there are other animals in the house food can be a source of quarrels. The 'dog in the manger' attitude applies to cats and dogs and if later in life your kitten is to use a cat door, saucers of uneaten food invite visits from his hungry friends.

As age increases and meals are cut out, a pup's or kitten's own feeding behaviour will usually tell you which meal is best omitted. He may be enthusiastic about food at every meal time but there will be some obvious preference. In very hot weather adult animals may not be keen on food during the heat of the day, and even a six-month-old kitten can appear not hungry at 4 pm when the temperature is in the high eighties yet ravenous at dusk when conditions are bearable again.

There are canned foods specially formulated for puppies and kittens, though somewhat more expensive than the ordinary foods. They are more concentrated and help puppies, especially those of the large breeds, to take in that extra nourishment that they require to fuel their growth explosions. Georgina's (my Staffordshire Bull Terrier) pups started on canned puppy food at four weeks of age. Perhaps kittens are helped too if they are fed this way, but my kittens (of unknown ancestry) have done very well on the ordinary canned cat food.

Every animal needs fluids as well as food, and they take it in various forms. Some cats – particularly Siamese and Burmese – seem to have an aversion to milk and will drink nothing except water. I think they are right. Cow's milk is an unnatural food for cats and dogs, and sometimes too much milk can be a cause of chronic diarrhoea. Lactose, which is the sugar in milk, is not broken down during digestion and this substance in the lower part of the bowel means that too many and too loose motions result. Moderation in all things is a good maxim, so not too much milk and none at all if bowel activity is excessive. A number of 'unreliable' cats become perfectly house trained once milk ceases to be their daily tipple. They were never dirty, just uncontrolled.

Make sure that drinking water is available at all times. There is no benefit from the lump of rock sulphur that used to be seen in every dog's water dish. Because sulphur is totally insoluble in water there is no point in removing it either, if your dog inherited a lump from his great grandfather. These blocks are eternal, that's why they are useless, sulphur never passes into the water and thus into the dog.

The position of a water bowl can be critical in certain circumstances.

Hairy, somewhat jowly dogs such as Cocker Spaniels may develop an eczema around their lips and in the folds of the jowls. This often starts because saliva dribbles on to the hair of the face and, like a teething child, scalds the skin around the mouth and causes a blistering effect. When a water bowl is sited next to the food dish the dog will drink and then nose out those last few morsels of biscuit. His wet whiskers, made more adhesive by some saliva already there, collect biscuit dust, and something close to flour paste forms around the lips. This dries and he feels sticky so rubs his face on the mat. Any slight chaps are scratched and the skin is broken. A scab forms and that tickles, so he rubs it again. Before long there is a nasty sore face – diagnosed, quite correctly as 'labial eczema' – but if the food dish had been ten feet away from the water so that the whiskers could drip-dry, the flour paste effect would not have happened. In the odd dog, this little thing can mean a lot. Dogs will always drink enough water, and so will most cats – except for the few that get into trouble with dry food. Worries about any dog or cat drinking too little are usually ill founded. Ultra-hot weather makes little difference; perspiration occurs only from the tip of the tongue and around the toes and leads to very little fluid loss.

Any increase in thirst can be an early warning sign of trouble. Kidney or liver degenerations, diabetes, cystitis and infections of the uterus are just a few of the ailments that lead to excessive drinking. How much any particular dog or cat drinks depends on many things, not least how much water is in his food, but if a dog that used to need his water changing because it became dusty suddenly starts to empty his bowl, this should alert his owner. No matter how well the dog seems, such a change in drinking habits warrants a visit to the vet if it goes on for more than three or four days. An early diagnosis might mean an early recovery.

Adult dogs and cats are quite content to stick to an unvarying feeding routine, but changes of feeding times disturb them, mentally at least. Most animals prefer to find that the food that they know has appeared on the menu yet again. Perhaps the desire for a variety of meals is one that we, as adults, have cultivated and all animals prefer a no change policy. Juvenile humans seem content with baked beans and sausages for ever. Some cats have changes of taste but an altered flavour of cat food usually solves this one.

When old age approaches, feeding needs changing again – more of this to come later in chapter 17 – but three or four (smaller) meals per day are often appreciated. The failing digestive system has less to cope with at any one time and the old animal has three or four high spots to enliven his day. Household scraps are always available, and are best used as part of the diet *in place* of meat, canned food or biscuits – not as well as.

10 · Obesity

Depending on which statistics one believes, somewhere between 30% and 60% of dogs are overweight. I don't know which is the correct percentage but there is no doubt that too many dogs are too heavy and enjoy life less because of this.

Edgar Rowsell, owner of a now slimmer dog, made the point of enjoyment much better than I could ever hope to do, when he wrote to report progress. 'You may be interested in the result of the diet that you suggested for our Corgi, Kandy. On April 9th 1985, just prior to being invited onto *Pets in Particular* (first series), Kandy weighed 42 lbs. I have weighed her today, December 12th 1985 and she now weighs 32 lbs.' (The book about Corgis that I read says she should really be 24 lbs. Considerable progress, but further to go yet.) 'The change in her life style has to be seen to believed. Although she was 9 years old last July she behaves like a dog half her age. She is very alert, loves her walks, never walks if she can run and is always ready to play and join in the usual family activities. No waiting for Kandy to catch up with everyone. Where before she just waddled along and took her time, she is now up with us or, as often as not, in front of us. We have a motto for her now, "Be lighter and therefore brighter" ... Kandy is not only healthier, more alert and happier but we will have her with us for several more years than we would have expected ...'

Perhaps less weight means a longer life, there is no doubt that it means a happier one. Part of ageing is that joints become less supple because the cartilage on the surface of the joints wears out. If the legs are carrying twice the weight that they were designed for, the wear and tear is greater and the older dog spends his last few years with each joint aching, not in pain, but never really comfortable. Walking is hard work, so he doesn't. That's boring so he eats to enliven the day, that means more weight, more ache.

Slimming is the solution to these problems, which need never arise in the first place. Obesity is not inevitable. Except for a very few disease conditions, the only reason for excess weight is eating too much food. Yet many owners do not wish to accept this fact. 'She's been speyed,' is an excuse from the owner, not a reason for a bitch being overweight. Any dog will put on weight given too much food, although a speyed bitch or a castrated dog will put on even more weight than the unneutered one. But neither will put on weight unless they eat more than their requirements. Just look at the next

Guide Dog for the Blind that you meet. All these are neutered, and very rarely is one overweight although Labradors are one of the greedy breeds to which all food is acceptable.

Guide Dogs can show any owner how to keep a dog with a trim figure. Each dog goes through life with a record book. This shows his age, when his next booster injection is due and notes any veterinary treatment that the dog is given. It also records his weight when he left the Training Centre. All Guide Dogs have a six-monthly health check from a vet – which all Vets do free of charge, and they are given booster injections if needed, which are supplied free of charge by the vaccine manufacturers. Weight is one of the concerns at this health check, and because Guide Dog owners are responsible, and an overweight Vet is going to see the dog at regular intervals, dogs weights change very little. A typical example is a dog that starts work around 18 months old and weighs 72 lbs. By the time he is eight years old he may weigh 76 lbs. Just over 5% for middle age spread is acceptable.

The important lesson is to weigh a dog at a year old and try to keep it close to this weight. Growth has finished and so the Corgi that is 22 lbs on its first birthday should be no more than 22 lbs on his second anniversary. If his weight is up to 24 lbs and carries on at this rate the dog will be 40 lbs by the age of ten. A two pound gain by the second year should sound alarms in the owner's mind, and the amount of food in the dog's dish should be reduced. That little bit of mathematics illustrates another important point: weight does not appear overnight.

Leaving this imaginary 40-lb Corgi let's get back to Kandy; 42 lbs when she was 9 years old. If we are generous she can be described as only 18 pounds overweight – all gained in 8 years (year one was growing, rather than expanding). That's a weight gain of roughly 36 ounces per year, about $\frac{3}{4}$ oz each week. An ounce too much food per day, say, two squares of chocolate each evening, explains this gain. If the owner decides after 8 years that his dog should lose weight, he tries to take off in 3 months what has taken 8 years to put on. When this does not happen many people give up in despair. But, as Edgar Rowsell tells us in his letter, it can be done.

Before any dieting starts, two things have to be established. It is essential to weigh the dog. Knowing the starting weight is useful, and a monthly weighing tells you if the excess is disappearing. The first pounds of weight loss are not obvious to someone who sees the dog every day. But the scales will record them, and show that there is hope of success.

Sometimes the difficulty of weighing provides a very persuasive reason for not starting a slimming regime. 'He won't stand on the scales,' is one cry. There is a simple answer. He doesn't have to. The owner stands on the scales, weighs himself, then picks up the dog and weighs himself plus dog. Simple subtraction gives the answer. The normal bathroom scales go up to

Weigh yourself first, then weigh yourself again while carrying the dog. Simple subtraction provides the answer. Kandy weighed in at 39lbs when she appeared on *Pets in Particular*. Today she is slimmer, lighter and brighter.

20 stone (280 lbs), thus any 12-stone owner can weigh a dog up to 8 stone in weight – one hundredweight, 112 lbs – which is as much dog as anyone can pick up and still balance on bathroom scales. There are difficulties when the owner is a little heavy. I cannot weigh any dog of more than 30 lbs weight without the pair of us going over the top of the dial. Very large dogs and overweight owners have to find larger scales or even a friendly weighbridge.

Knowing the pet's weight is useful on other occasions too. Worm tablets are usually given on a weight basis, and if the dose is one tablet per 10 lbs body weight it is much better to know the weight exactly rather than guess it. There is much less need for cat weighing, although it is nice to know that the tablet dosage is completely accurate, but the 'cat in arms' system works very well.

Because an overweight dog must have eaten too much food it helps to know how much is too much and many owners get a shock when they work out what their dog does eat on a typical day. Sometimes the food in the dog's bowl is the smaller part of the daily intake. Add up the dog food. One way of getting this answer right is to work out how much is bought. If he's supposed to eat 4 ozs of biscuits per day and a 3-lb bag normally lasts a week, someone's calculations are astray – or there are some very fat mice about. Don't forget the extras, titbits, bribes, rewards or what ever they are called. The bit of toast at breakfast, a sweet biscuit for elevenses, the scraps at lunch time, some tea in his bowl at 4 pm (mainly milk, and sugar to taste), plus a piece of chocolate each evening and a few more biscuits to go to bed with make a considerable heap of calories. Put one day's extras into a polythene bag. It may be surprisingly full.

Slimming starts by reducing the food to two thirds of the previous amount, and the best way of keeping to this diet is to make a bag of biscuits last as long as it should. At 3 ounces per day 3 lb of biscuits should last sixteen days. If they are all gone within a fortnight, three or four biscuitless days should follow. The dog cannot understand why he's being starved and I sympathise with him, but the owner is to blame.

It is very easy to say that all titbits and rewards should cease when weight loss is the aim, and its dietetically correct, but heart breaking for the dog. No one loves him, no one cares, what has he done wrong to warrant such deprivation? It is often better to subtract the extras from his normal food and continue to give tiny rewards. A half sweet biscuit instead of two, one chocolate drop instead of six.

Less food means less bulk, and a being-slimmed dog can feel very empty. Not only is this unpleasant for the dog but it might tempt him to go on a begging round and have half-a-dozen snacks each day from animal loving neighbours. Boiled cabbage and raw or cooked carrots can be added to his feed, purely to provide extra bulk. Vegetables are quite unnecessary in a dog's diet and there is little or no nutritional value in them. They pass through the dog almost unchanged – which is quite obvious by a passing glance at a carrot-eating dog's motions. But the dog thinks he's had a good meal. If a dog gets a taste for carrots, and perhaps pieces of apple, the tit-bit problem is solved. No need for any restrictions so long as carrot or apple is involved.

All slimming is a family affair and it is no use Mum dieting the dog if Father or Grandfather continue to give fattening extras. But they can give vegetable extras *ad lib*, and remain popular with the dog and Mum.

After a month of restricted food, weigh again. If a pound or so has gone there is no doubt that a more shapely dog is about to emerge. If there is no weight loss, someone is cheating – or the dog is eating elsewhere. Reduce the food in his dish to half the normal amount – he can't be starving to death while he remains overweight. Once food intake is less than the body needs, fat reserves are used – which is another name for slimming.

As soon as a dog feels lighter, he becomes more active, 'lighter and brighter', and more energy is used up which, by itself, has a weight-reducing effect. When a dog is back to a proper size, he may need more food because the reserves are used up and a larger food intake balances supply and use of energy, and makes for a constant-weight dog. But continue a six-monthly check on the scales so that any future increase can be stopped after the first pound.

11 · *Vaccinations*

People are living longer nowadays and so are pets. A major reason for this increased life span is the use of vaccination to prevent infectious diseases, which used to kill many youngsters.

No vaccine in animals or man is 100% perfect but the present-day dog and cat vaccines are extremely good, and while one still hears of the odd case of disease in an innoculated animal, such failures are rare and many happen because the vaccine was given at the wrong time.

There is more to vaccination than using the syringe as a dart and the dog or cat as the board. Injections must be given at the right age into a healthy pup or kitten, which must then be kept away from any natural infections until the vaccine has become effective.

Vaccines work by making the animal develop its own protection against a disease. Thus there is a time lag between injection and reaching a level of resistance sufficient to prevent illness developing if infection occurs. Immunity developed within the animal (known as acquired immunity) is long lasting, although as time goes on it wears out. Hence the need for 'booster' injections.

Immediate protection is given when antibodies made by another animal are injected. This 'passive' immunity lasts for a few weeks only because it is just borrowed, and not home made. Nature has been using this method since time immemorial to make life safer for all newborn mammals. Mother's milk contains antibodies to whatever infections (or vaccinations) she has experienced. The youngster absorbs these during suckling and so has some protection when he leaves the germ-free safety of mother's womb and meets a variety of germs including some potentially harmful ones. Bottle-fed pups, kittens, lambs or calves may be less able to resist neo-natal infections because non-natural milk does not contain these invaluable antibodies.

Solving one problem often creates another – and Nature's way of protecting the newborn creates difficulties when it comes to immunisation. If a kitten or pup is vaccinated while the maternal antibodies are present in any significant amount, they will interfere with the vaccine and prevent the development of immunity. Injection too early in life is one of the reasons for vaccine 'failures'.

Passive immunity rarely lasts more than a few weeks and as pups and kittens are normally weaned by six weeks of age, they should be free from maternal antibodies by 10 weeks. Most are, but the odd one is not. Most vaccination schedules consist of two and sometimes three injections at fortnightly intervals. One reason for this timing is to make certain that if the earliest injection was a little too soon and maternal antibodies interfered with it, the later ones would be fully effective because enough time had passed to allow any passive immunity to wear out.

Now to the practical aspects of vaccination, although I am not apologising for the theory that came first. The correct vaccination procedure varies with the vaccine, the amount of infection in the district, the previous disease history of the dam, and the kennels she lived in. The best advice about this must come from the vet who is going to do the injections. He knows what vaccine he is using, he knows the local disease patterns and, if the puppy or kitten is from a local breeder, he may know something about the kennel history. If an adult dog from a rescue home is being vaccinated, knowledge of any infections in those kennels helps in choosing the best injection schedule. The worst possible advice is from some breeder 100 miles away, or a doggy friend who always followed her father's advice. Maybe that vaccine used that way was correct in another county, and the best possible three decades ago, but times change, and local, up to date advice is best.

Dogs are protected against four major diseases:

Distemper: which includes Hard Pad. This is a virus infection, and causes a flu-like illness, with coughing, sore eyes, discharging nose and some diarrhoea. This goes on for six weeks or so. Better one day, not so well the next. The dangerous time is usually late in the illness, when the infection may spread into the nervous system and cause fits or paralysis or a continuous muscle twitch called chorea. These nervous complications appear in about half the cases and very few of these recover. It is a terrible disease, heartbreaking to treat because after weeks of nursing, just as recovery seems likely, fits might happen and all the effort, and all the dog's misery was to no good purpose. Because vaccination is so effective we are inclined to forget distemper. Anyone who started dog owning twenty-five years ago may never have seen an infected dog, but when I started practice we would see a dozen or more cases every day, and half of them died. There are a number of localised outbreaks each year even today, almost always in unvaccinated dogs, although a few older dogs, injected as pups, but that have never had a booster, succumb too. I'm still afraid of distemper.

Infectious hepatitis is another virus infection involving the liver. It is not a very common infection but in the acute form it causes death after an illness of very few hours. Less acute infections may lead to a damaged liver – and a shorter life expectancy.

Leptospirosis is a bacterial infection. There are two types, one mainly in the liver, the other affects the kidneys. The disease is spread in the urine of infected dogs, rats or many other animals. Treatment by antibiotics is effective if a diagnosis is made at an early stage, but even after a recovery some damage to the kidneys remains and later in life may show itself again. It's much better to prevent leptospirosis than to treat it.

Parvovirus: or more specifically canine parvovirus. The name simply means small (parvo) virus and there are many different parvoviruses in various species of animals. The canine one appeared as a totally new disease in 1978. It causes an acute gastro-enteritis with considerable vomiting and an intense depression in dogs over eight weeks of age. In very young puppies there was severe damage to the heart muscle and when the disease first appeared, sudden death from heart failure in a seven-week-old puppy was an all too common happening. As the infection spread, breeding bitches began to develop antibodies to parvovirus and passed this immunity to their pups, via the milk. Thus young puppy infection became a rare occurrence, and heart damage is now quite uncommon. However, the infection is still very much with us and older pups and fully grown dogs are at considerable risk unless they are vaccinated. As with almost all virus infections there are no drugs that will actually kill the infection in the dog and treatment is mainly designed to combat the dehydration that continuous vomiting causes. No matter what efforts are made, many dogs still die from parvovirus. Another example of protection being better ...

When the first cases of parvovirus arose there was, of course, no vaccine available. No one makes a vaccine against a disease that is not known to exist. The cat disease feline enteritis is also caused by a parvovirus. Not the same one as in dogs, but a close relative. This relationship saved the lives of very many dogs. There was a vaccine against feline enteritis which was injected into dogs and gave a very effective immunity to many of them. Now, parvovirus vaccine made for use in dogs is even more effective, but dogs and dog owners should be grateful to the cat vaccine (and the manufacturers who increased production at very short notice) for helping to prevent what could have been a major threat to the dog population throughout the world. The other extraordinary feature of the start of canine parvovirus was that the infection appeared in the United States, Europe and Australia almost simultaneously. I can't explain, I just wonder.

Cat vaccination covers two major infections:

Feline enteritis: this virus causes an acute illness leading to death within twenty-four hours in the worst cases. Some of the reports that one reads about cats being poisoned are based on an outbreak of this disease. The characteristic signs of intense depression and constant vomiting are similar to what would happen with certain poisons. Although feline enteritis is caused by a feline parvovirus there is no possible chance of an infected cat transmitting the disease to a dog, or vice versa.

Cat flu is caused by two viruses, with or without superimposed bacteria, so the signs vary. In general the death rate from flu is low, but a significant number of cats can be left with a chronic catarrhal infection which causes them to sneeze, cough and splutter for the rest of their lives. Not nice for the cat, and it's not nice to have cat that is forever sneezing around the house.

While most vaccines are given by ordinary hypodermic injection, one cat flu vaccine is administered as droplets into each nostril as is one of the vaccines against kennel cough (an infectious bronchitis) of dogs.

Which vaccine and when, is something to decide upon with your own vet's advice but, as a guide, a new puppy might be given his first injection at ten weeks of age, another at twelve weeks and perhaps a third at eighteen weeks. Some breeders have their pups injected at six weeks of age to protect them against any infections that might be brought in by adult dogs visiting the kennels. This does not mean the pup has had his vaccinations, it simply means he has had one injection as part of a whole programme.

As soon as a new puppy, or adult dog arrives, phone the surgery and ask about vaccinations. Then go on from there.

Cats normally need two injections only and these should be given between 10 and 14 weeks, with a fortnight interval between the two injections.

Vaccines should only be given to completely healthy animals. The dog or cat has to respond and make antibodies. This process will work best in a fully fit animal that is not having to devote its energies to coping with any other infection. For the same reason many vets prefer to allow a pet to settle in its new home for ten days or so before starting any preventive injections. There is a certain stress involved in coping with a change of diet, change of home and routine, and the strongest immunity might not develop while this is going on.

Unpleasant after effects from vaccination are almost unknown in dogs and cats. Sometimes there is a day or two of sneezing after the nasal method, but the general joy of living and eating should be unimpaired.

The protection produced by the vaccine is long lasting but not everlasting and the level of immunity falls over a period of time. If natural infections are about, antibody production is stimulated and protection is reinforced. However it is difficult to find out if any individual pet has met up with such a natural boost to his immunity and so we give artificial boosters in the form of another dose of vaccine at regular intervals, usually annually. It is quite possible that many boosters are wasted because there has been a bit of natural infection about. Blood testing could tell us this but an extra injection can never do any harm and is no more costly than a blood test would be, and most pets hardly notice an injection.

When the course of injections is complete, your vet will give you a certificate to that effect. Read this before you leave the surgery. Make sure that the details are complete and that you know when the booster vaccination is due. When that is done, it will be recorded too. Keep the certificate in a safe place. You'll need it, either for a show or if your pet has to be boarded. Reputable kennels insist on an up-to-date certificate before they will take any dog or cat. If you find a kennel that does not worry about certificates, it may indicate that they don't worry about anything and are best avoided.

Costs of vaccination vary depending on which particular course of injections is used and veterinary fees in general vary throughout the country. There is no fixed scale of fees, nationally or locally. Think in terms of £20.00 for a course of injections for a twelve-week-old puppy or kitten. Don't be afraid to ask the cost when you phone to arrange or enquire about vaccination.

12 · Neutering

At least 200,000 dogs and cats are destroyed every year because no one will give them a home. That alone is a good enough reason for considering neutering a bitch or she-cat. It may be better to find homes for those unwanted animals instead of destroying them. There are always dozens of offers to adopt a dog or cat that has featured in some tear-inducing newspaper or TV story, complete with 'Ah' pictures. I am not convinced that someone who decides to take on an animal, just on impulse, even a kindly impulse, is any better than the impulse buyer of a puppy at Christmas time. Neither of them has thought it through.

I'm not trying to discourage anyone from breeding from their pet *by intention*, either because they want to perpetuate that strain, or because they know that every pup or kitten will be bespoke before it is ready to be weaned. Pet over-population results from accidental litters or misguided ones because pregnancy is supposed to 'do the bitch good'.

If fewer puppies and kittens were born there would be less destruction, and the most effective way of population control in dogs and cats is by speying females. That statement does not prove that I am a male chauvinist (perhaps I am) but just that every time a she-cat is neutered a couple of dozen kittens, or more, are not born. There are very sound reasons for castrating male cats but population control is not one of them. If a tom cat is neutered this simply reduces the competition for females, and all the un-neutered toms are grateful.

Let's look at the pros and cons of neutering – females first. There is the obvious advantage that pregnancy is prevented. One of the many old wives tales implies that one litter is an advantage and in some strange way the bitch or she-cat is fulfilled having given expression to her maternal instincts. I think this is total nonsense and a good example of anthropomorphic reasoning, when human feelings and thought processes are attributed to animals.

Heat is prevented too. There is no need to keep a bitch imprisoned for three weeks, twice a year, and there is no damage to the garden as a result of half a dozen hopeful suitors settling their quarrels amongst the flower beds – and cocking their legs everywhere else. It is very difficult to confine a cat on heat except in a purpose-built cat cage. She will escape from the average house sooner or later, and pregnancy is almost certain. It is possible to prevent heat by the use of hormone injections or tablets and this is very useful when a planned litter is intended next year. After the hormone use is stopped, normal heat cycles resume. This method is not a lifetime solution. If breeding is never intended, speying must be the best answer.

Another old-wife story about speying is that it alters the character of bitches in particular. Depending on who is telling the tale it causes either nervousness, aggression, stupidity, obesity or skin trouble. Again utter non-sense, and Guide Dogs are good evidence to support my view. They are all speyed and it would be difficult to find better-balanced, friendlier, more intelligent dogs, with good figures and sleek coats. This particular myth started as an owner's excuse. If an uncontrolled, highly nervous bitch is speyed she will remain uncontrolled and nervous and if she bites it is because she is frightened and knows no better. The owner has not the enthusiasm or inclination to train her and so it is easier to blame speying rather than himself.

Blaming the operation for everything that happens in the future can go to extremes. One lady would not consider having any cat speyed ever again because, as she told me, 'The last one was run over by a bus afterwards.'

Middle-aged bitches (un-speyed) may develop pyometra (an infected uterus) and treatment means a hysterectomy to remove an enlarged and diseased uterus from a seriously ill bitch. Speying removes both ovaries and uterus and so pyometra cannot occur. This is not a major reason for speying, but it is a slight pro.

Any operation involves some risk. Modern anaesthetics and surgical techniques reduce the danger element to very small proportions but one or two bitches and one or two cats will die during operations this year and the next. But then one or two dog and cat owners will have motor car accidents while they are taking their pet to the surgery for operation. The two risks are about equal but this is a very small contra.

Every vet has his own views about the best age for neutering. I prefer a bitch to have had one season before the operation. This usually means that she is approaching a year old, maybe older. By this time bone growth has finished. In a puppy the bones of the legs consist of a long shaft and a lump at each end held in place by a plate of cartilage. Growth takes place at this junction of shaft and epiphysis (that's the lump). When the animal becomes an adult the cartilage disappears, the shaft and epiphysis fuse together and growth stops. Early neutering (either sex) delays this union and so the bone goes on growing and becomes longer than usual. This effect shows itself most commonly in cats. The one that was castrated or speyed at four months develops into a very large, long-legged adult. By contrast a she-cat that became pregnant at seven months and was then speyed after her litter was weaned remains a diminutive cat. Pregnancy speeds up the fusion at the bone ends, so growth is completed earlier than usual.

There is another reason for waiting until a bitch has had one season. This makes certain that full sexual development has occurred and the vulva is at the rear of the bitch rather than high up, inside the thighs, as in a puppy. If the bitch grows up without this change she may suffer scalding inside the thighs because her infantile shape in this region means that the urine splashes on the skin. Not a very common problem, but it is too late to change things when it has happened.

Female kittens are best speyed at six months plus if the first litter of kittens is to be prevented. Cats can be speyed after they have had a litter. I prefer to wait until a fortnight after the kittens have left. This allows Mum to recover from the strain of feeding hungry youngsters. She-cats come on heat again soon after the kittens go and another pregnancy may start. Operation is still quite possible and it may be better to operate on a slightly pregnant, fully fit cat than to hurry and do it when she is still 'one degree under' as a result of the last litter.

Now males. Almost all pet tom cats are castrated, and an unaltered tom is often only a partial pet. Delightful when he is at home, but he is inclined to disappear for days and weeks at a time when it's Springtime (January to June in a tom cat's calendar). When he does return, he smells. Tom cat odour is distinctive and all-pervading. Castration removes this stench. There is also a high possibility that the wandering tom cat returns when he is feeling less than fit because of an abscess, due to fighting. Cat bites, which are puncture wounds, become infected because germs are driven deep into the tissues, the wound closes over at the surface and infection is left imprisoned. These germs multiply and a painful abscess forms, sometimes life-endangering if blood poisoning supervenes. All cats are potential abscess victims but toms fight more than she-cats and so develop more infected bites.

The best age for this operation? Ask your vet for his advice. My view (but take his), is around eight or nine months. Old enough for bone development to have almost finished, but young enough to avoid the smelling and wandering-off age, and again physical sexual development is nearly complete. This means that the cat has a full-size urethra – the tube from the bladder to the outside world. Crystalline deposites from salts in the urine are troublesome in a few cats (see p. 49) and may block the urethra so that urine cannot be passed. A full-sized tube is less likely to suffer this obstruction than a small bore one which is the sexually immature state.

While castration of cats is a routine procedure and has given a very special meaning to the word 'doctoring', this operation is less usual where dogs are concerned. They are the odd animal out, because, apart from humans, dogs are the only domesticated species where non-neutered males wander at large. Few stallions are kept as riding horses, and bulls are treated with great respect and not allowed into fields through which a footpath runs, except for beef bulls accompanied by cows or heifers. No one in their right mind turns their back on a billy goat, and a reputedly meek sheep can be a raging monster in the form of an angry ram.

A few working dogs are castrated to 'keep their mind on their work'. Guide Dogs and working sheep dogs fall into this group, and it must aid concentration when every passing lamp-post and tree is not an invitation to sniff to see if 'she' passed by. Operations are done for particular reasons in individual dogs. Hyper-sexed dogs can be a nuisance and embarrassment by reason of their activities with cushions and anything else that is available. This dog's wanderings in search of sex makes him a danger to himself and any other road user. If he is kept in monastic seclusion with only his thoughts for company he becomes a very frustrated animal. Over-aggressive dogs that fight every other dog they meet can be reformed by castration and a reduction in the amount of male hormone in their bloodstream. The dog that fights every other canine, regardless of sex, is not likely to be changed by castration, Original sin motivates him.

Castration is sometimes used for therapeutic reasons. Tumours called anal adenoma, that arise around the anus of middle-aged dogs, will regress quite considerably after the dog is castrated and enlarged prostate glands which trouble old dogs, return to normal size when the dog is neutered. Growths sometimes arise in the testicles and castration is necessary to remove such a tumour.

The preferred age for 'routine' castration of dogs is around one year old, when bone development is just about complete. Castration for behavioural or therapeutic reasons may take place at any age although one must be certain that the old dog is being offered a fair exchange, in so far as he should be expected to benefit and gain enough enjoyable life in exchange for accepting the upset of an operation.

All these operations are done under general anaesthesia and there is very little post-operative upset. Apart from some drowsiness from the anaesthetic almost every dog or cat is back to normal activity the day after the operation.

The actual nuts and bolts (if that's not an unfortunate phrase) of the operations involves removing the ovaries and uterus in females and removing both testicles in the male. Sterilisation by ligation of the fallopian tubes or by a vasectomy is not the same thing as neutering. In animals one is trying to prevent both reproduction and sexual activity and so the manufacture of sex hormones must be stopped by removal of those glands – ovary or testicle, that make such hormones. Costs vary as ever, but the sort of figures to have in mind are about £50 for a bitch spey, £18 for a kitten and rather more if she's pregnant, around £10 for a tom cat castration and £30 for a dog – unless it's a man-eating Rotweiller or similar when it could cost a lot more. Again, ask your vet.

A final word, to men only. I have been writing about dogs and cats – and that is all. It is amazing the number of times that a wife arranges for the dog or cat to be castrated and the husband phones to cancel the appointment.

13 · Bad behaviour

Behavioural problems occur at least as often as those from disease, and when they do, an owner who would like to change things does not know where to go for advice. There are a few animal behaviourists, and there are of course vets, who would be more than willing to help if owners only thought of asking them.

There are dogs that have booster injections with commendable regularity but no one mentions that this thoroughly immunised dog is an utter menace in the car. Let's stay with that dog. The excitable one is very eager to get into the car, then sits whimpering waiting for the journey to start and begins to bark and scream, working up to a crescendo which either culminates in sickness because of hyperexcitement, or results in saliva-covered windows, seats and floor. Your dog Mrs Er . . .?

Whoever's dog, he has been trained to behave like this. Inadvertently trained, perhaps, but there is a very high probability that this dog has been taken by car to some open space where he can have an exciting and enjoyable run. After a dozen trips the dog learns that anything to do with cars equals galloping about, which is very exciting, and anticipation knows no bounds. The owner's relatively feeble remonstrances have started too late in the development of this behaviour pattern, and before long patient resignation sets in. 'He's a marvellous dog, but . . .' Owners can be remarkably patient.

Reformation is possible. Start by walking him on a lead to his place of exercise (it will do you both good). If at all possible come home by car and let the journey end without excitement. Try to teach the dog that car journeys are dull, nothing happens when they finish. Don't, for example, feed him as soon as you return. If he has spent a couple of years learning that car trips are exciting, it is going to take many months to unlearn and re-learn. The lesson can be reinforced by teaching him that you (who he should think of as pack-leader, and if he is not so convinced, training will be very difficult) are delighted when he sits quietly on the back seat of a stationary car. Play this game with him, simply sitting on the back seat of a parked car with the door open. After two or five minutes sitting still, congratulate him – not too effusively, that's more excitement – calmly but unmistakenly. For every one out of ten good behaviours some tit-bit reward is justified, but again given with as little excitement as possible. Try to progress to a closed car door, then you sit in the front seat while the dog remains in the back. Starting the engine is the next test and finally try short journeys round the block and back, still giving low-key and muted congratulations.

There is a very real prospect of this dog changing into a 'nice to have in the car' type, after some months of lessons. But it needs effort and not just pious hope. I received one letter about a six-year-old dog that bit the postman. The writer asked, 'Would he grow out of it?' Time would certainly solve this one, but only when the dog died. With a lot of hard work reformation could be possible in life, but hope alone is useless.

Another car problem is simple sickness and this can usually be solved if the dog travels often enough. Any dog may be sick during his first car trip which is why I believe that it is so important that every puppy should, if at all possible, learn from a very early age that car trips are part of every-day living. But if one disastrous journey means that the dog is 'protected' from further travel thereafter, he will almost certainly be sick on his annual car ride. (Midshipman Nelson was seasick on his first voyage. If he had been kept on dry land because of this, what would have been the result at Trafalgar?)

There may be a place for travel-sickness tablets or tranquillisers in a few cases. Always ask your vet – human remedies might not be suitable, and the tablets for a neighbour's dog could be the wrong size for yours. I'm anti-tablet: they disguise rather than cure, and any tranquilliser leaves a dog that little bit dopey, somewhat slow in his reactions, which is not helpful at the journey's end if he has to cope with unfamiliar surroundings. A very tranquillised dog might be so much at peace with the world that he ignores road dangers until it's too late. Much better to spend time training. It works. An owner of a bad-travelling Golden Labrador, sick before the first mile, was persuaded that familiarity with the car might work. I suggested she took the dog for a 200-yard car journey first thing in the morning, with instructions that if there was no sickness or excitement, to increase the distance day by day. Never has my advice been acted upon in such a literal manner. The owner got out of bed, put on a dressing-gown and thus attired set out with the dog in the car. She lived close to a motorway. By the beginning of month three she was driving seventeen miles along the motorway and back again, still in dressing-gown and nightie while the dog caught up with its sleep on the back seat.

Aggresive dogs may be so because of their basic make-up. Certain breeds guard instinctively, and it is no use blaming a dog when he behaves as his nature dictates, when he has never been shown any alternative. Other dogs are aggressive because they have never been taught, or allowed to socialise with people or other dogs and so react from fear of the unknown. Every dog is territory conscious and has to be taught that people from outside his family may be allowed into 'his' territory. No dog will ever 'grow out of' aggression. the best answer is not to allow such behaviour to start, but if it has, the owner must re-establish, or more often establish for the first time, control of his dog. Aggression towards the owner and family is very difficult to stop if it has been in existence for many months. The dog is boss and the owner is frightened, which reinforces the point of not allowing dominance to start.

At the first sign of a dog becoming possessive over a bone, his toys or an arm chair, TAKE ACTION. Take the bone or his toys away from him. Give them back later and, at a time of your choosing, remove them again. If necessary, put the dog on a collar and lead in order to control him while his playthings are given up to his pack boss. In the same way, he must leave the arm chair when he's told to do so – on a collar and lead if that is the only way. When the bad habits start, there is only a mini-battle to be won, not much more than a skirmish. When bad habits are established, a long and serious battle is inevitable.

Although I have just used military terms, there is little need for physical fights with the dog, and no place for physical punishment in order to 'teach him a lesson'. He will learn from a beating, but only to bite first, and hard, before there is any chance of being punished. Voice, and cold disapproval is enough after any misbehaviour. Congratulations after reformed behaviour are much more effective.

Dog-training classes are an extremely helpful and perhaps essential part of dog reformation. Not because the classes themselves rehabilitate the offender but because the owner learns to control the dog, and in many cases attendance at the class means that the dog meets people and other dogs and becomes accustomed to, and even bored by, their company.

Give the training classes a chance. Plain commonsense should make it obvious that a dog's attitude, built up over a year or two, is not going to be changed in one lesson or even two. I often receive letters from people who have been to training classes for three weeks 'and he's no better'. Resolve to go for six months, and be prepared to do some homework. Every delinquent dog is impossible at the first few classes and his owner is usually reduced to tears, rage or acute embarrassment. After six months of hard work there is every chance that the same owner will feel seven feet tall, insufferably self-righteous and superior because their dog is now well behaved. All of a sudden, they are quite unable to understand how anyone could own a dog that behaves as badly as the Collie belonging to that lady who came for the first time last week.

If an owner learns no more than the capacity to make their dog sit, stay and lie at command, many problems are solved. If a barking dog is told to sit he may well stop. Few dogs bark while sitting. If he is one of the few, tell him 'down' – no dog barks lying down. The experience of attending classes, mixing with people and dogs, along with a new found confidence because the dog no longer fears the unknown, may well have stopped much of the needless barking anyhow.

Once a better behaviour pattern starts, consolidate it. Five minutes per day repeating the lessons is time well spent. The dog thinks that it is a game, but he's continuing to learn.

Damage to house furnishings and decorations is another common misdemeanour. In some cases the dog is left alone for such long periods of time that he just has to find something to do, and no one can blame him. And the situation won't change except by finding a more suitable life-style for the dog. In other cases a doted-upon dog behaves like Attila the Hun when he is left for an hour or so, while at other times he is perfect. The 'doted-upon' may be the key. The dog is so attached to his owner that he cannot bear to be parted from him (or more usually her). The stress of parting is so intense that the dog does some damage, just to express his feelings. When the owner sees the damage, the dog is told off, but in such a gentle way that it might suggest congratulations.

There are two parts in stopping this vandalism. Make certain that all partings are 'cold' ones. Let the dog feel that perhaps it is not quite the adored animal that it might have supposed. Thus parting is less stress and the pet's reaction may be more subdued. It is also wise to attempt to show the dog that good, non-destructive behaviour is appreciated. Train him to be left. Shut the dog in the kitchen for ten minutes or so, then, if all is peaceful, let him out and congratulate the good behaviour. Keep up with such 'games' for weeks on end and the destructive dog may reform, and the dog that barks when left alone might realise that there are rewards to be reaped as a result of staying silent.

Simple protection of the house and furniture can be achieved by buying a travelling or sleeping cage for the dog. These are all wire cages, big enough to allow a dog to lie comfortably in any position, to stand upright and to turn around freely. It is not unreasonable to shut a dog in such a cage for a few hours, or even overnight. The house benefits.

Such a cage can often help toilet training. Few dogs will ever soil their own bed, and if an unreliable dog is confined each night for three months there is a very good chance that he will be a clean dog thereafter. This confinement must only be used when there is no doubt about the dog's health and well being. If wet nights are a result of any disease condition and the dog is not able to control his bladder, it is quite wrong to use such a cage. That dog needs treatment rather than training.

The larger pet shops sell such cages and they are displayed at many Dog Shows.

Attending classes will improve a dog's behaviour, and many problems are solved if an owner learns no more than how to tell his dog to sit, stay and lie.

One other dog misbehaviour, which is remarkably common but nobody likes to talk about it, is coprophagia: the eating of their own, or other dogs' faeces. I have heard very little about this habit from clients in the consulting room, and have never, I think, been asked about it on any radio phone-in. But most weeks one or two letters arrive from people both disgusted and distressed by this aspect of dog behaviour (writing is all right, talking about it isn't).

First, I would point out that such behaviour is not abnormal, and second that it is generally harmless to the dog and is not a sign of vitamin or mineral deficiency, worms or even less speakable vices. It is just a bad habit of dogs, which, like most bad habits, is learnt by mimicry from kennel mates and occurs much more often in dogs in large kennels than in house pets. Puppies taken from kennels at four or five months of age are more likely to show this vice, simply because they have had more opportunity to learn it.

Another cause may be over-strict toilet training. If a puppy is punished every time a mess is found, and even worse if his nose is rubbed in it – a sort of Dotheboys Hall training, then puppy learns that the greatest crime is to be found out. He passed the motion several hours ago and so cannot associate his punishment with that act. If he eats his motion, his owner will not find it, therefore pup is not unpopular. Perfect dog logic.

There is no need to accept this habit and dogs can be trained to behave in a more socially acceptable fashion. Keep temptation out of the way, which means clearing up any faeces as soon as possible – a good practice anyhow. Secondly, teach the dog that you are pleased when he ignores any faeces. Take him towards it, on a lead, and tell him to walk past. When he does, congratulate him and sometimes give a tit-bit. Many lessons later he'll look for praise or the tit-bit and forget past sins. There are certain tablets that make faeces appear foul tasing to the dog. Ask your vet about this way of helping to break the habit, but remember to use tablets as well as training, not instead of.

Just as an aside, and a very good example of the dangers of treating all species in the same way, all rabbits eat some of their own droppings. They pass two types. The hard pellets that every rabbit keeper knows, and a softer variety that usually arrives through the night. These soft droppings are eaten by the rabbit as his major source of Vitamin B. The bacteria in the intestine make the vitamin, but because this happens at the lower end of the bowel, it has to be re-eaten in order to be absorbed while passing along an earlier part of the digestive tract. So don't try to reform a rabbit.

Behaviour problems in cats are less common. Either they are paragons or not easily found out. Clawing at furniture, carpets, wallpaper and door posts distresses owners (and the furniture). It is a perfectly normal cat habit applied in the wrong place. Aversion therapy, by the use of a water-pistol, will direct the cat to acceptable scratching places. If the cat discovers that he gets a sudden wetting whenever he starts to extend a claw in certain directions, he will associate the wallpaper or furniture with the wetting and begin to avoid it. A small water-pistol discharges about a tablespoonful of water so there is no danger of damaging furniture or the cat, and the owner's relationship with his pet is unharmed too because the cat thinks the three-piece did it.

Another type of spraying is when some cats mark their territory by urinating on convenient (for them) sites within the area. This is normal tom-cat behaviour and one of the reasons for neutering cats is to stop spraying – and the extra nuisance of tom-cat smell. Any cat may spray if he or she is disturbed and stressed by competition from another cat or any frightening circumstances close to its territory. If a new cat or dog comes to live in the house, or next door, stress is created. A nasty fright from a pasing tom cat or even a near miss from a motor car might make a cat feel insecure and trigger off the instinct that says 'mark my boundaries'.

It has been said that 25% of cats will show spraying behaviour at some time in their life. The cat is not being 'dirty', and punishment will not alter things at all. In most instances spraying stops when the trigger factor goes away – or becomes part of the normal scene and no longer a threat. But no one wants to live in a house with damp patches while waiting for a natural conclusion. Tablets or injections of a hormone similar to the one found in pregnant animals often solve the difficulty. The cat feels pregnant, placid, at peace with the world, and certainly not prepared to worry about any extraneous happenings. This therapy can be used in male or female cats, neutered or not. The tablet is a prescription-only medicine and has to be obtained following advice from your vet.

A cat that has had a nasty experience in the back garden may be frightened of appearing outdoors and feel even more vulnerable while he is digging a hole and squatting thereon. So, thinks the cat, it's safer indoors. If this happens try giving him a toilet tray in a box similar to the old fashioned dog kennel so that there is privacy and protection, as well as dry litter to dig in. If a cat persists in passing motions at one particular spot indoors, try feeding him in this place. Cats do not soil feeding areas.

Whenever house training fails, for whatever reason, a thorough cleaning of soiled areas is essential. After washing, use some mildly smelling disinfectant. The whole house does not need to smell of carbolic, which is very poisonous to cats. Their sense of smell is sensitive enough to detect a fragrance which we would not notice.

Kind-hearted owners become concerned when their cat goes hunting and brings back trophies for display on the back doorstep, or even on the hearth rug if he is given a chance. The cat is offering a tribute to his owner, he is being a totally normal cat, not cruel, fierce or greedy. I know of no way of stopping cats from hunting, and owner over-reaction to the trophies might only serve to encourage the cat to think he's doing the right thing.

Other people's cats appear to be very badly behaved; they fight, while your cat of course, only ever defends himself. When next door's cat digs holes in your seed bed, water is one repellent in this case, and a hose pipe can be helpful. Dead holly leaves spread on the ground also deter cats, as does wire netting, but both look untidy. I am told that tiger droppings are also effective and rather obtrusive but first find your tiger!

14 · If only . . .

Minor mishaps and major tragedies often happen for very simple reasons, and when the metaphorical (and sometimes literal) post-mortem takes place, 'If only . . .' is one of the main findings.

Many a silly accident would not have happened if only the dog had been on a lead. It is never safe to allow any dog on a road that carries motor traffic unless it is on a lead – attached to the dog by a secure and well-fitting collar. Some owners take a pride in allowing their dog to walk at heel, at all times. 'No need for a lead with Prince,' they will say. I have seen the mangled body of many a Prince, who for once saw something out of the corner of his eye, and forgot all that training. He was half way across the road before anyone realised – too late. Every vet knows a different variety of the same owner. There is the owner whose dog does not even need a lead when visiting the vet because he is quite certain that his dog will not fight while waiting in the reception area (perhaps not, but he may cock his leg and irrigate the door post). In unusual circumstances any dog might panic for a moment and either take a snap at something or someone, and it is a very stupid human vanity that risks his own dog's reputation rather than admit that a lead could be useful.

A significant number of dogs die each year as a result of poisoning from slug pellets. It is worth emphasising that one pellet here and one pellet there in the garden is enough to kill a mollusc. Slugs and snails do not have to fall over a heap of pellets and break their necks. For a dog, two pellets do not constitute a fatal dose, but two ounces or more may. That is why the packet of slug pellets in the garden shed or the kitchen cupboard can be so dangerous.

Rat poisons are less dangerous if tiny baits are used, and safer still if it is placed in the middle of a narrow drain pipe – wide enough for any rat, but impossible for any dog. Again the can of poison left without the lid may be a fatal invitation to a curious puppy.

Pills for human use are then eaten by animals and pups, of course, are the commonest culprits. Any variety goes down with equal alacrity. Contraceptive pills, indigestion tablets and Granny's green ones too. Child-proof containers are not dog-proof. Not only can a dog tear the plastic apart and swallow the pills, he may eat the container as well.

If any poison that is swallowed can be removed from the dog within a few minutes, fifteen at the most, there is a high probability that no untoward signs will appear because the toxic material will not have been absorbed by the stomach. A crystal of washing soda (sodium carbonate) makes an effective emetic to induce vomiting. A piece the size of a walnut is needed for a Labrador-sized dog, but only about half this size for a small Jack Russell or a cat. Simply give the washing soda as if it were a pill. Within five minutes vomiting results and whatever was about to do serious damage is out of the stomach. There are more sophisticated emetics that your vet can give by injection but time is of the essence. However, two minutes spent phoning your vet for advice before doing anything would not be an undue delay.

If signs of illness have appeared it is too late for emergency vomiting treatment. At this stage knowing what poison is involved could be the most important matter. There are many different vermin poisons, dozens of weed-killers and garden insecticides and Gran's green pills may contain many different drugs under the sugar coating. Take the bottle or container to the surgery when you take the dog or cat. Small print will almost certainly define the contents and once the poison is known a specific antidote may be available. When pest-control firms are active in your neighbourhood, ask them what poisons they are using. Write the name down, and the name of the contractor. This information could save an animal's life, and prevent the usual cry of, 'If only we had thought . . .'

There are some common playtime accidents worth knowing about, and so avoiding. Throwing sticks can cause trouble. Dogs can impale themselves on sticks two or three feet long. The dog chases the stick and dives at it, open-mouthed when the spinning stick is nearly upright, with one end touching the ground. The other end is driven down the dog's throat and may do extensive damage to the roof of the mouth or the soft tissue of the neck. If it is a brittle stick and a piece breaks off while embedded in the cheek, the consequences might be even more serious. One-foot-long sticks or mini-logs are much safer, but be careful not to hit the dog while throwing to entertain him. Golfers have been known to hit their dog either while swinging or when he appears in the line of the ball's flight, and even French Cricket can be dangerous when batsman and dog aim for the ball at the same time. Avoid purchasing small rubber balls sold especially for dogs which are of a size to wedge in the back of the throat and choke the dog. I've seen more than one death and a dozen or more emergency removals, just in time. Tennis-ball size or larger is safest. Beware of anything smaller.

Fishermen hook their dogs – and other people's – so cast carefully, while cats may be hooked by well-tied flies or fishermen's hooks brought home while still baited with a mackerel strip.

Cats and puppies swallow needles, but only when the thread is still attached. The wool or cotton is the attraction; the needle the danger. Most needles penetrate the back of the mouth or travel straight through the digestive tract and become wedged at the anus on the way out. It's very painful, and the dog or cat shows this by straining and crying when it hurts.

If a piece of thread is protruding from either end of an uncomfortable pet, one that is choking or straining for example, DON'T pull the thread. To do so may cause pain, but much more importantly the thread is the guide line to the needle. By following the thread your vet can find and remove the needle relatively easily once the animal is fast asleep under anaesthetic. A needle without thread is as difficult to find as the proverbial one in the haystack. Best of all, always un-thread, and it won't happen.

On page 75 I said that carbolic acid was dangerous to cats, and this warning applies to a whole group of tar/oil and cresol-like compounds. Creosote itself can be fatal if a cat gets any quantity on its coat or feet. Paraffin, turps, diesel oil and even some skin dressings suitable for humans and dogs will kill cats by absorption through the skin. So one golden rule is: if in doubt, don't use it on a cat. And if a cat has become covered in any potentially dangerous subtance, clean it off as soon as possible. A mixture of clipping and bathing is the best way. Washing-up liquid, children's hair shampoos (non-medicated) and ordinary toilet soap are safe cleaning agents. Swarfega is safe too and helps to remove heavy oil and tar. Continue washing and rinsing until the smell of the contaminating oil has disappeared. Dry with towels and a hair drier. The cat won't enjoy any of these ministrations but he'll survive them and could die without them.

Dogs are much less sensitive than cats but if they get paint, oil or tar on their coat or feet, never use turps or paint strippers to clean them. These will blister and irritate the skin and the cure may be worse than the trouble. Swarfega, soap or shampoo and water are the only safe cleansers.

15 · Vets – and how to treat them

I have already said 'Ask your own vet', 'see your vet', a good many times. Perhaps it is time to talk about *finding* 'your' vet and what you can reasonably expect from him. Wise owners start looking for their future vet when they start looking for their first pet.

Personal recommendation is best, so ask your animal-conscious friends who their vet is. Then telephone him, even before getting the new kitten or puppy. Ask about vaccination ages, surgery hours, appointments or open surgeries. If you have any doubts about the pet you are buying, or about your own ability to 'vet' it, the first consultation will be a check-up of a potential pet.

Stay with one practice. You may not see the same individual vet every time – although it should be possible to arrange this for non-emergency visits – because vets have families and need time off, so in an emergency the vet on duty has to be accepted.

Nowadays most examinations are done at the surgery. More facilities are available and help is at hand. It is possible to see dogs at home, but owners are not always the best handlers of their pets, and kitchen tables do not often have a light of the quality of an examination lamp above them, and the largest estate car in the world cannot carry everything that is available at the practice premises. House visits take very much longer than surgery consultations, three or four times longer, and as the larger part of the fee may be for the veterinary surgeon's time, visits cost more, and much of that extra is for car driving and time spent before the animal is even touched.

House calls and emergency treatment are things you could well discuss with your new vet at an early stage. Every practitioner is under an obligation to provide a twenty-four hour service to cope with real emergencies, but it is worth knowing in detail how to use such a service if you need it.

After the first six months in practice, every vet has been told, 'I think it is marvellous, animals can't tell you anything, it must be much easier for a Doctor.' I'm not sure about that. If a patient is determined to mislead, the medical man would need to be a mind reader to sort things out. If pets cannot speak, owners can, and good information from this source is invaluable. The first thing that any vet needs to know is why the animal has been brought to him. We don't ask, 'What's wrong?' because this invites the very clever response, 'That's for you to find out,' which does not get things off to a good start. 'Why' is vital. For vaccination? Because he's scratching? To be destroyed? Perhaps the owner is just worried about some little thing that has happened or has changed. This last reason is a very good one and there is no need to approach your vet in an apologetic fashion. 'I'm sorry to bother you, it does seem trivial, but . . .' If vets weren't bothered they would starve to death, and it is a perfectly proper use of veterinary time to ask about anything animal, even if the answer turns out to be that there is nothing to worry about.

Pets often arrive with the whole family, and this is perfectly proper, but there have been times when I have wished that the family could agree on something about their dog. Father says that it is fourteen, mother says ten – not a vital matter – but when mother says it hasn't eaten for a week and father says, 'No dear, I gave him some meat this morning and he ate the lot,' this contradiction is important. Five minutes later it emerges that the meat was eaten, but vomited immediately so mother didn't think it counted, and in any case she had to clear it up because father went off to golf. It is almost time to phone the Marriage Guidance Council.

The more detailed the history of an illness, the better the diagnosis, so it is worth trying to clear things in everybody's mind first. Kennelling dates and the time of the last season can be confirmed at home, with calendars and diaries to help. Questions like 'When did you first notice the lump?' can be answered precisely if auntie noticed it when she was staying – and there is agreement as to the time of her visit.

Don't be afraid of asking questions, and don't be embarrassed. There is no reason why you should know the difference between a tumour, a growth, a cyst and a neoplasm. They are only words which mean more or less the same thing. If you are worried about the possibilty of your pet having cancer, ASK. We are not mind readers. If the thought never crossed our mind because it is so ridiculous to suspect a cancer, we cannot know to say that there isn't one, unless you ask. I did learn in my later years in practice to recognise an expression on owners' faces which meant that this question was in their mind, but was not going to be asked. A fixed expression of disquiet, a reluctance to say anything, and the consultation is incomplete as far as the client is concerned. 'There's no reason to think of cancer', or any words to that effect, change the atmosphere completely. Relaxed smiles and a sheepish, 'Well I was worried'. How many people go away still worried, I do not know, and others don't even consult their vet because they are afraid that he will give them bad news – a euphemism for some malignancy. Knowing won't alter anything, and finding out that there is nothing to worry about makes the sun shine on a foggy day.

Decide to some extent what you, as an owner want. Your vet can only ever advise. You have to decide. No vet will ever seize an animal from you and destroy it. The excuse that, 'I didn't take him to the surgery because I thought he would be put to sleep,' is utter rubbish. Obviously only a very selfish and uncaring owner would refuse to have a pet put down if they were advised that it was quite inhumane to keep it alive. But that is an extreme example.

Extensive treatment might be required but be impossibly expensive. This problem is increasing, not because owners are willing to pay any less, but because advances in medicine and surgery mean that things that were utterly impossible 20 years ago are now quite feasible with today's modern techniques but that the costs preclude them. Heart pacemakers are a case in point. They can be fitted to dogs, and work very well, but usually the pacemaker has been donated. Otherwise the cost could have been in excess of £1000.

It is possible to insure to cover veterinary fees. There are several companies offering this cover and most vets have details of the different policies. Read the small print – as with any other insurance policy – to find which one suits you best. In passing, one of these policies is a most acceptable Christmas present for an elderly relative who dotes on her animals and worries about the costs. She can then go to the surgery without counting the pennies too closely.

Take time to ask questions when deciding on treatment. If an operation is advised, often the decision can wait until tomorrow, after a family conclave. When a decision is desperately urgent the advice is usually so unequivocal that it presents little difficulty – although you have the right to disregard it. Most decisions will wait for a short time. If any explanation is not clear, or you feel that you need more information, ASK. Answers cannot always be absolutely definite. We are dealing with living animals and nothing is certain. There's no such thing as a 100% guarantee. Unexpected things happen. Anaesthetics are very safe, but not 100% safe, and the occasional dog or cat will die unexpectedly while being neutered in some surgery this year – a rare happening which is no consolation to the owner, or the vet who is equally upset.

We are often asked about the chances, 50%? 80% This really means nothing. The answer might be more accurate if 100 or 1000 animals are involved, but the question is about one dog, cat or whatever. That one is either 100% alive or 100% dead.

When difficult decisions have to be made there is one other question which I think is fair. Ask your vet what he would do if this was his pet.

No vet knows all the answers to every question but they do know more about animals than you and are often well able to find out what they don't know.

16 · Worms, fleas and other parasites

Every animal has its parasites, generally specific to one or two species and parasite control is an important part of good animal keeping.

Fleas are ubiquitous but choosey about their host, and unless life is very hard, they stay within a selected group of species. Dog and cat fleas are totally interchangeable. The fleas are called Ctenocephalides canis and felis, but as they cannot read, either pet is an equally good feeding ground. Oddly, a marked geographical distribution occurs: north of a line from Liverpool to the Wash most fleas are dog fleas (even on cats); south of this line there is a significant preponderance of cat fleas.

Both species look exactly the same to the naked eye, flattened side to side, dark mahogany in colour, quick moving while on the dog or cat's skin, and great jumpers when off the animal. They are about half the size of a grain of canary seed.

When a dog or cat starts excessive or unusual scratching a search for fleas should be the very first investigation. It has been written that 90% of skin troubles in cats and dogs are linked to fleas. I'm not sure that I agree with 90% but I would settle for 75%. Even if fleas are not the primary cause of some skin trouble their presence will make a tiny itch into a significant one. If it is a recent infestation it can be difficult to find one of the four or five fleas on a pet. While you look at one bit the fleas might move to another. The best way of searching is to use a fine comb along the spine, finishing at the tail root. Look for fleas on the comb. If no fleas have turned up, look again for tiny black specks, not unlike coal dust. These are flea droppings, and a very simple test can prove that the cat has not been sleeping in the coal box. Put the black specks on to a piece of wet, white tissue-paper. Leave them for five minutes and a brown stain will appear around each granule, showing that this is partly digested blood that has passed through the flea. And it is your pet's blood – another reason for attacking every flea. Because flea-dirt remains stationary it is a much better indication of infection than relying on finding the parasite itself, and no droppings are a good guarantee of no fleas.

Rabbit fleas are quite distinct although they turn up on rabbit-hunting cats, clustered around the tips of the cat's ears, the lips and eyelids. Some times there are so many fleas that the cat's ears and lips look as if they are outlined by make up pencil.

Birds have a particularly large flea – usually restricted to wild birds only – but this species can be a nuisance when young birds leave their nests. The fleas are abandoned in the nest, and sooner or later have to set forth in search of food. They can appear in bedrooms (from nests in the eaves) and might, in desperation, bite people as well as animals. This is usually a short-lived problem, solved by most of the fleas starving to death. Fleas are very uncommon in domestic poultry, caged or aviary birds, and, MOST IMPORTANT, never use any of the dog and cat flea-sprays containing choline-esterase inhibitors on birds. They kill the bird too. If in any doubt, read the instructions on the can, or ask your vet, but don't take a chance.

Caged pets, such as guinea pigs, rabbits and gerbils are rarely affected.

Control of fleas on dogs and cats depends on attacking the flea at all stages of its life cycle. The only fleas on the pet are adult ones and, after mating, the female flea lays her eggs in dusty places (such as the cat's box, the dog's bed, down the arm of a chair or beneath the carpet). The eggs hatch in as short a time as sixteen days if it is warm enough, the first stage being pupae which later turn into young fleas. At this immature stage they feed on dust and their own egg cases. Under the very best conditions (for the flea) an adult may develop by twenty days after hatching. If conditions are not very inviting the young fleas may remain, semi-dormant for as long as a year.

Before fleas can breed they must have a feed of blood and that is when they arrive on the animal. In the whole lifetime of a flea, relatively little time is spent on the dog or cat. When fleas are permanent cohabitants it is said that there are fifty fleas somewhere in the house for every one on the pet.

Killing the adult fleas by using dusting powders, aerosol sprays, shampoos or medicated soaps is one line of attack. Even more important is the use of something to kill the fleas before they reach the animal. The same dusting powders may be used on the pet, but better preparations are those made especially for young-flea control. Some kill the larvae and others simply stop the young fleas from reaching adult life, so that they never feel the need to feed from the pet.

There is no need to treat the whole house, unless you own twenty flea-ridden cats. In the one- or two-dog, or cat, household it is possible to delineate their snoozing spots: box and basket, of course, the front door-mat in hot weather, the patch by the radiator where they sleep, and the piece of carpet that the sun shines on in the morning. It was either Talleyrand or Napoleon who said that time spent in reconnaissance is seldom wasted, and this is equally true when fleas are the enemy. Dust or spray these selected spots once a fortnight for at least twelve weeks. Regular washing of any dog or cat blanket helps too – a modern washing-machine programme is lethal.

Newspaper as bedding, and cardboard boxes to sleep in, make control easier. Simply burn and renew every week.

As with any other medication *always read the instructions* when using any insecticide. Twice as much, or twice as often, will not kill twice as many fleas, and it might make the pet feel less than fully fit.

Many owners say that their cat will not tolerate an aerosol spray. This might be true in a very few intances but the vast majority will, if made to. As with all cat handling, put the cat on a table with a smooth surface and hold him by the back of the neck, head pressed down very slightly. Then squirt. The instructions for one much-used aerosol say 'up to three seconds spray' for a cat, which is not a very long period for a cat to be upset, and he isn't if properly handled.' Some cats will salivate profusely immediately after spraying. The same cat may salivate during an attempt to give him a tablet, and even if he's put in a basket and taken to the vet. Excitement is the cause of the salivation, not the aerosol.

There are also tablets which pets can be given to attack fleas. The insecticide is excreted on to the skin and kills the fleas in that manner. It is one way of making sure that there is no untreated area anywhere on the coat.

Flea collars contain insecticides which are said to rub off on to the fur. When one asks for more details of how they work there is a certain confusion in the answer. No matter, there is no doubt that collars do work, particularly in killing that first flea. Fleas have to come from somewhere and the previously un-infested cat most often collects the mother of his future fleas by sleeping in a strange bed in the summer months. Perhaps on that heap of sacks in the garden shed, which is also the resting place of the big ginger tom that calls round. His fleas have laid eggs on the sacking and the next generation are waiting for their feed of blood. The next cat to lie there is fair game.

Poorly-run kennels are another source of trouble, although many cats arrive for boarding already well laden with fleas. A collar will kill these fleas before they have a chance to breed, always providing the collar is still active. The collars have a life of about ten weeks (read the instructions again). I am not enthusiastic about collars if toddling children are about. If sticky fingers grasp the cat by its collar, and then the same fingers are used for eating the lollipop that made them sticky, some insecticide could also be eaten, which might not be a good thing. People are sometimes bitten by dog and cat fleas, and certain individuals seem to attract much more than their share of flea bites, particularly fair-skinned blondes. I'm not certain that the flea makes this specific selection or if that particular type of human skin is hypersensitive and so shows a spectacular reaction, which can be very distressing.

A hard-hearted, but obvious solution, might seem to be to get rid of the dog or cat that is blamed as the 'source' of these fleas. I have known this advice to have been given by doctors. If it is followed, the bites will increase in number very quickly because the fleas have been deprived of their major feeding place – the animal – and the only other warm-blooded creature available is the now pet-less owner. Keep the pet, get rid of the fleas.

Another version of this flea-feeding behaviour occurs in an empty house that was home to pets and their fleas. When the place is deserted and there are no suitable mammals to bite, the young fleas go into a state not unlike hibernation. Vibrations from footsteps waken these sleeping beauties, and so when an estate agent arrives to survey the house that has been deserted for many weeks he is fair game for all the re-activated fleas. On at least two occasions I have supplied flea sprays to young gentlemen who did not care to return to their offices until the effects of the spray had restored them to a state of comparative comfort.

Purchasers of houses such as these can save themselves and their pets trouble (and bites) by having the house fumigated while it is empty. It can be a DIY effort, using malathion smokes. Commercial pest-control companies will undertake this work and the Environmental Health Department of the local District Council may be prepared to help, and will certainly be able to give technical advice.

Lice are another skin parasite. Less common than, and totally distinct from, fleas. The essential differences are that lice breed on the animal and most lice are relatively immobile. They spend much of their life attached by the mouth to the skin of the host, feeding by sucking blood. Lice are usually found on the ears, head and neck of dogs, over much of the body in cats, and around the neck and along the spine towards the tail in ponies and donkeys. Lice are about the same size or a little larger than a flea, brown in colour, but when the louse is fully fed its abdomen assumes a bluish-purple shade because of the blood therein. The front part of the sucking louse is buried in the pet's skin but it is often possible to see its three pairs of legs just behind the attached mouth parts. Nits are the eggs of lice. They are khaki-brown coloured and may be seen stuck on to the hairs of the coat.

Most of the insecticides that are used against fleas will kill lice also, but nits are very difficult to kill. Thus louse control depends on killing the adults, then re-treating so that the young lice, which have hatched from the nits since the first treatment, can be killed before they have lived long enough to produce their own crop of nits. Ten days is the magic interval. All existing eggs should have hatched in that time and none will be old enough to breed. Two sprays or dustings are enough in theory, but it is much better to treat every ten days for four treatments so that if the odd one escapes it is caught next time. Lice spend very little time away from their host but a thorough clean-up of bedding and box makes sense and might avoid a re-infection. Insecticidal baths are useful in long-haired animals. Dusting powders do not always reach the skin when there is a thick and matted coat above. A soapy shampoo has a penetrating effect and reaches those parts that other insecticides do not.

All dogs and cats living together must be treated whenever flea or louse control is attempted. If one is left, because he gets so upset, or because he was not scratching, or just because he wasn't at home at the time, much of the effort is wasted. Fleas or lice will certainly be reduced in numbers, and everything will operate better for a time, but the whole routine of treatment will have to start again within a few months. The aim is elimination of these parasites, not just population control.

Each species of louse lives on one species of animal or bird. There is very little movement from one host species to another. Many hundreds of different lice live on wild birds but each selects one bird species only.

Lice on pets must be controlled for the pet's sake – they cause intense irritation but there is no danger that the pet's owner will be affected in any way.

Ticks are the largest of the blood-feeding parasites that appear on animal's skins. The commonest tick, found in urban cats and dogs, is the hedgehog tick. They vary in size from a lentil up to a large baked bean, depending on the age of the tick and how long it has been present on an animal. Ticks hatch from eggs laid in dry scrubby sites and climb up the vegetation waiting until they can attach themselves to some passing animal or bird. The tick then hangs on by its mouth-parts and feeds on the animal's blood. As it feeds, it engorges – hence the size variation. The newly arrived tick is dark mahogany in colour, the fully fed one has a grey-blue abdomen extending from the dark-brown body of the tick. After about ten days the fully fed tick releases its hold, falls to the ground, moults and then climbs up the grass to wait for his next victim. This process is repeated three times before the tick is mature.

They are indiscriminate in their choice of host. Sheep ticks will infect, and kill, grouse on the moors. Cattle, rabbits or dogs are equally at risk and under farming conditions ticks spread several diseases by reason of their blood-sucking life style. Pet animals usually suffer no more than acute irritation in some cases. Some cats react violently to ticks and are quite dangerous to handle because the tick seems to cause pain in some way. Another cat might have a dozen ticks, scattered around the skin of his head and neck and is oblivious of these passengers.

Ticks are best removed, but never by pulling off. The head can be left embedded and this might cause an abscess. There are various methods of making the tick release its hold. Smothering it in butter is one – the tick cannot breathe. Holding a cloth soaked in concentrated salt solution over the tick is another – this withdraws water from it. Meths on a cloth is also used – presumably to intoxicate.

If ticks recur during the summer months, an insecticidal shampoo every fortnight will leave enough residue on the pet's coat to kill new ticks on arrival before they can attach themselves. Although dog and cat infections are often caused by ticks that really wanted to find a hedgehog or a fox, don't feel that fox or hedgehog persecution is an essential part of protecting your pet. It's not necessary, a bath every fortnight will do.

There are other parasites that live on animal skins but are too small to be seen by the naked eye. Treatment of such infections can only follow a proper examination and diagnosis. There are many causes of scratching in dogs and cats, and unless fleas or lice can be found, DIY treatment of skin troubles is no more successful than picking the Derby winner with a pin.

Early treatment of itches is essential because scratching causes more scratching, and self-inflicted damage may be more serious than whatever caused the original itch. See your vet when there's a little itch, and so stop the big one.

There is one mite infection of birds that is fairly obvious and unmistakeable. This is scaly face, common in budgerigars. The cere, which is the blue or brown area above the beak and around the nostrils, is the area involved and the smooth surface becomes scaly and thickened. Damage will extend on to the face and the beak itself, often causing abnormal or uneven growth of the beak. The cause is a mite called Cnemidocpotes which is easy to kill by painting a suitable insecticide on the affected area with a camel-hair brush. Your vet or a good pet shop can supply the correct treatment. A similar mite of the same family causes scaly leg in domestic poultry. No prize for guessing that in this infection scaly areas appear on the birds' legs and feet.

Worms come in all shapes and sizes. They are selective in their host species and seldom cross from one species to another. There are two types of worms in dogs and cats: roundworms and tapeworms.

Roundworms are so called because they are round in cross-section. The adult worm looks rather like a piece of plastic-covered wire, between two and six inches long, curled or even coiled as a spring, and pale beige-mushroom in colour.

The worms live in the intestine of the host and eggs are passed out in the faeces. The eggs develop in moist warm conditions and are swallowed by another dog. Once inside the intestine, the worm larva leaves the egg and burrows through the bowel wall, into the bloodstream, and travels through the liver, into the lungs, up the wind pipe only to be re-swallowed and returned to its starting point in the dog's intestine. Then if it meets a worm of the other sex, they mate, eggs are laid, and the next generation start this extraordinary journey.

There are several significant consequences of this migration. Some of the larvae stop part-way through their journey and encyst, often waiting for years until something happens which will tell them that it is worth starting to travel again. If a bitch is pregnant the larvae may divert through the placenta and arrive in the unborn puppies. Thus puppies are actually born with worms and encysted larvae wake up and re-start their journey when pregnancy hormones stimulate them.

It is very easy to get rid of worms in the intestine of dogs and cats. Roundworm tablets, given in the correct dose for the weight of animal, are highly effective and the results can be seen in the shape of dead worms, passed in the two or three days after worming. But larvae travelling around the body or encysted in the tissues are difficult to catch and repeated dosing is necessary to kill worms as they become adult. There are drugs which will destroy encysted larvae but these should only be used following your vet's advice.

Migrating larvae can be a risk to human health. Rarely, very rarely, children swallow an infected egg of Toxocara (that's the dog roundworm). The egg hatches and the larva begins to migrate. In many instances the larva dies because it is in a strange host. Other times it gets lost and does not follow its normal route. Larvae may travel to the human's eye and cause damage to the retina which leads to impairment of sight to a greater or lesser extent. Such eye damage, mainly in children, is diagnosed in up to fifty cases per year in the United Kingdom. Not many when compared to the figures for road casualties but one case is too many and each case is an avoidable heart-break for the child and family concerned.

If only (again) every dog owner would worm their pet for roundworms every six months these fifty cases would be reduced to five in a very short time and the whole danger could be eliminated in a few years. Because worm eggs are not infective until the larvae have developed for about thirty days, infection may be present in any park or open space frequented by dogs that carry worms, and any child can be open to the hazard, dog owner or not. Worming your own dog is essential, but this alone does not protect your children.

In general, roundworms do little harm to adult dogs, but they can be a cause of serious diarrhoea and other ailments in young puppies. This is another reason for regular worming of all dogs and especially for worming any bitch, both before mating and at an early stage of pregnancy.

Tapeworms affect all species and every tapeworm has at least two hosts (some have three or four). The commonest tapeworm in the dog and cat is Dipylidium caninum. Nearly completely harmless, but very unpopular with pet owners who do not like to see the melon-seed sized segments crawling around the rear end of Tiddles or Betsy. These segments are pieces from the tail end of the tape worm and are full of eggs on their way to the outside world looking for their intermediate host. The cream-coloured segments dry up to become shrivelled pale-brown egg cases. The eggs are shed, and in the case of Dipylidium, must be eaten by a flea or louse if they are to carry on the next part of their life cycle.

Once in the flea, the egg develops into a cyst stage and if the flea is then swallowed by a dog or cat, the cyst forms the head of a new tapeworm and the next generation has started life.

Every tapeworm has a similar 'double' life. There is another tapeworm in cats that has voles or shrews as the intermediate stage. They eat the eggs and the tapeworm cyst develops in the little rodent and when a cat catches and eats a vole the tapeworm cyst is eaten too, and a new worm can start to grow. Tapeworm tablets will kill adult tapeworms. They will not kill the worms that are about to appear either from co-habiting fleas or voles that are victims of a hunting cat.

Flea control is essential if Dipylidium tapeworms are to be removed, once and for all. The rodent-spread tapeworms are an intractable problem. Cooking would help by killing the cysts, but I have yet to find a cat that will put his mice in a micro-wave. Regular dosing is the only solution. Fortunately, these tapeworms are merely unacceptable to the owner, they do little harm to the cat.

One very small tapeworm of the dog is detrimental to both human and animal health. It is a little four-segment worm called Echinococcus. This worm lives in dogs, and sheep are the intermediate host. Swallowed eggs develop into large cysts (containing up to a gallon of fluid) in the liver, chest or abdomen of the sheep. They may cause death, and dogs are reinfected by eating carcases containing these cysts. If the tapeworm eggs from the dog are swallowed by a human being the large cysts develop just as in the sheep, causing 'hydatid disease' which is always serious and may be fatal. Major surgery is required to remove these cysts. Now, all the above sounds alarming, and rightly so, but the worms are very limited in their distribution and occur solely in farm dogs in a few limited areas of the country where large-scale sheep farming takes place on mountains or moorlands. For the worms to survive, dogs must have access to sheep carcases and the same dogs must be free to roam – and pass motions – on grassland that will be grazed by sheep. Parts of the Pennines, the Scottish Highlands and some islands, and the hills of Wales are troubled by this particular worm – and nowhere else. In Powys, a scheme has been set up to worm all dogs within a large area in an attempt to eliminate infection. Not only is the worm becoming much less common in farm dogs, but human infection is beginning to fall and sheep health has improved. Farmers, vets, doctors and the pharmaceutical industry who have joined together to make this scheme work, and make life better for sheep and people who live in mid Wales, must feel very satisfied with the progress so far.

Birds, tortoises, snakes, horses, sheep and goats have tapeworms too. They're relatively harmless but well worth removing. Make certain that the correct worm dose for that particular animal or bird is used. What is safe for one is not safe for another, so read instructions and ask first.

Grazing animals such as ponies, goats and pet lambs need worming for redworm and similar tiny worms, too small to see with the naked eye but which live in their hundreds of thousands in the stomach and intestines of various herbivores. All these worms have an uncomplicated life story. Eggs are shed on to the pasture (at the rate of hundreds and sometimes thousands per gramme of faeces), where they develop for a few days and are then eaten during grazing. They then become the next generation of adult worms.

Whenever animals live in close proximity to others, worm populations can build up very rapidly and regular worming is essential. Every month in the summer and every two months in the winter may not be too frequent for urban ponies.

Worm doses come in many forms, pellets for feeding, powders for dusting and even injections. They are all effective if used properly.

There are many other parasites as well as those I have mentioned, but this is not a text book on parasitology. Suffice it to say, 'Little things mean a lot,' whether one is referring to little attentions or little crawly things.

17 · Old age and beyond

There are two certainties in our lives, death and taxes. Animals are not pursued by Vatman or the Gannets from the Revenue, but death remains the inevitable end to their lives.

Life spans vary from species to species. The Biblical 'three score years and ten' translates, roughly as:

Dogs: between ten and fifteen years. Little dogs live longer than big ones. The giant breeds are senile by ten. Some few tiny dogs reach their twentieth birthday.

Cats are old by the time they are fifteen. Odd ones manage twenty and the sixteen-year-old cat turns up more frequently than a dog of the same age.

Ponies go on into their thirties, and many twenty-year olds are working and becoming wiser and better schoolmasters for their young riders as each year passes. Donkeys manage to live longer – maybe because they put less effort into each day of living.

Birds vary considerably. Little finches live to five, six or seven years. Canaries and budgies might reach early teens. Parrots sometimes pass the half century. Laying hens can live until seven or eight years of age (although breakfast will be eggless for most of the year if the poacher pan has to be filled by such an old lady).

Little furry mammals in cages have life spans very much in proportion to their size. Mice and hamsters manage two years on average. Rats and gerbils three plus. Guinea pigs six or more, and rabbits might become teenagers.

Fish, especially cold water fish, may have very long lives. The Carp's life is measured in decades.

Tortoises are handed on from one generation to another and certainly pass our three score and ten. Other cold-blooded pets, such as snakes, can live for a very long time, and the last series of *Pets in Particular* revealed something about the life span of snails. One Roman Snail that appeared had lived with its present owner for the past five years.

Wild animals and farm animals never reach old age. When wild animals become slightly senile and unable to compete for food and territory they are killed either by predators or their own kind, or they starve to death because they are too slow to hunt.

Farm animals have to be profitable to the farmers and when they reach

Life spans vary from species to species. One of these snails had lived with its owner for five years. *(Below)* Tortoises are handed on from one generation to another.

a certain age this profitability reduces and so their place is taken by a younger, more productive replacement and the old one goes for slaughter.

Apart from man, only the protected and cossetted pet has to face the problems of old age, when physical powers fail and, in the seventh age, the circle is complete. 'Last scene of all, that ends this strange eventful history, Is second childishness, and mere oblivion, Sans teeth, sans eyes, sans taste, sans everything.' Man or animal, if life goes on long enough, the results are the same as they were when *As you like it* was written.

No one can reverse the ageing process. Those bits and pieces which go to make up a living body all wear out with time and while one worn bit might be replaced, senile decay is when everything disintegrates at the same time.

It is possible to help old animals enjoy the latter part of their lives by changing their routine a little. Give the old dog or cat several small meals each day instead of the one or two that he had while in his prime. Four snacks per day means that the digestive system can spread its work out through the whole of the twenty-four hours and will be able to cope better. The dog has four 'high spots' to look forward to, and four reasons for a stroll outside afterwards – which might help to delay any senile incontinence.

Old dogs need a sleeping box that allows them to lie stretched out in any direction. The small box that he enjoyed curling up into, causes stress to ageing joints which nowadays don't take kindly to being compressed into strange positions. The large cardboard box that a television set is packed in makes an excellent sleeping place. Earlier I recommended a box on its side as a sleeping place for a tiny puppy, and said that he felt secure with a roof over his head. When an old dog goes into that second childishness and primitive fears and insecurities assert themselves, walls on three sides and a roof overhead can be just as comforting as they were fourteen years earlier.

Treat aged cats in a similar way, more and smaller meals, safe and secure sleeping places. Groom old cats, even if they are impatient of your attentions. They may not take as much care over their toilet as they once did – stiff joints prevent some of the acrobatics that self grooming demands – but cats have a pride in their appearance regardless of age, and the clean and tidy cat feels that there is still life in him.

Although these little attentions make life more comfortable for old pets, they do not prevent the inevitable. Wear-out goes on; weakness becomes so severe that the old dog cannot get to his feet without assistance; the old cat can't climb up to her chair. Weight loss increases but this is typical of senile decay. Very old people shrivel, so do very old animals.

Everyone hopes that their pet will die naturally, at the end of a long and happy life. 'Natural' death is unusual. Sudden death from circulatory disease is uncommon, except in turkeys, but this might be because man has bred weaknesses into certain strains of this bird. The old animal goes on living, getting thinner, less active and possibly more miserable day by day. In the wild, Nature would have 'put him to sleep' by starvation or with the help of some other animal which would kill the weak and defenceless one.

No matter how much we protect and preserve a pet, the time comes when deterioration is accelerating and life should end. The owner has to decide when 'enough is enough', and most people find this a very difficult decision and some avoid making it. I think it can be very simple if one considers the pet's pleasure and enjoyment of life and nothing else. There is just one question. 'Is he still enjoying his life for most of the time?' Look back at his week. If he (dog, cat, pony, rabbit, it matters not) has a miserable ten minutes getting to his feet on Monday morning, and seemed unhappy for half an hour on Thursday, but the rest of the time he slept well, ate well, seemed pleased to see us, and went for a little walk every day, then life still offers something. Short periods of being less than content are outweighed by an otherwise general inerest in daily living. If there is five minutes rheumaticky pain once or twice a week, but the remaining six days, twenty-three hours and fifty minutes are pain free, it seems quite reasonable to ask the dog to put up with this short-term pain – and relieve it with tablets if possible.

Owners often ask, 'Is he in pain?' as if this was the only thing that mattered. Of course, we cannot ask any pet to endure continual or acute pain, but the odd ache is another matter. I don't believe that we should ask any pet to endure life at all when the pleasure of living has gone and this would always be my criterion for deciding when life should end. When the old animal is waiting for death he is tired, bored, slightly miserable, and probably frightened because he feels weak and his primitive instincts tell him that he is vulnerable. He may wag his tail, but only just, or purr quite loudly, but these may not be signs of contentment, they are more likely to be signs of fear – peace signs saying, 'I am helpless, don't attack me, I mean no harm to you.' A slight wag or a purr, are not reasons for prolonging life when every other sign from the pet says that living holds no pleasure any longer.

This terminal misery can last for weeks, which is why it is so often wrong to 'let him go naturally'. The last good turn that anyone can do for a pet that has lived with them for many years is to take away those miserable last few days or weeks of life.

In a pet-keeping lifetime every owner will have to make this decision four or five times, simply because the natural span of a cat or dog is so much less than ours. It is an owner's decision. Your vet can and will help you, but that does not make it any less difficult when the occasion arises. I can write and talk about someone else's pet quite coherently and logically, but I have been as indecisive as anyone else when my pet is the one in question – and I don't expect to be any better next time.

When any animal is to be destroyed there are a number of practical questions that arise. Without a doubt the best method of euthanasia is by injection of a gross overdose of barbiturate anaesthetic into a vein. This is literally 'putting to sleep'. Almost identical drugs are used for normal anaesthesia, and dogs that have to be aneasthetised several times show no apprehension the third or fourth time round. This leads me to the conclusion that there are no painful or unpleasant sensations connected with such an injection.

Although it is the best way, there are limitations. Injections into a vein are not always easy ones, and in old animals with poor blood pressure they can be very difficult. Injection is easier when there is good light and the animal is held still. This often means that conditions are better at the surgery on a good table with a shadowless light and a nurse who is experienced at holding animals for injection.

Home or surgery is a decision that you have to make with your vet, but make it on the basis of what's best for your pet rather than pandering to your own sentimental (or even selfish) feelings. Don't force your vet to try to inject under poor conditions to satisfy your whim. Animals which have come to the end of their life are not very bothered about where they are, or by a journey of a few miles. A tranquilliser may be given by simple injection under the skin. When this sedative has had half an hour to work, the more difficult injection can be given to an animal that is oblivious to panic and cares little about who is holding him, and where he is.

It is possible to inject cats and small dogs into the abdomen, aiming for the liver or kidney, and these injections are almost as rapid in action as injections into the vein. Every vet has his own preferred methods and techniques. Leave it to him and let him decide on the best way of giving your pet a peaceful end. Remember that the pet's feelings are paramount, yours matter much less.

The final decision to make concerns disposal of the body, whether it is to be buried at home, or an animal cemetery, or cremated. Undertaking is not really a vet's job, but because no one else is responsible we do try to help. Most vets can dispose of pets they have destroyed. Some can dispose of pets that have died at home or been killed in road accidents, but there are some physical limitations. Incinerators may not be allowed in city centre locations, some district councils undertake disposal of carcases, others will not, and commercial firms have to be employed. Some councils incinerate, some bury on tips.

It is not a satisfactory situation, and remains so because of the good will of most vets in making some arrangements to help bereaved owners who are sometimes even more upset about finding a last resting place. Anyone who does feel strongly about the final disposal should talk it over with their vet well in advance, even years before. Find a dog cemetery, find an animal crematorium so that there is no need for a distressing search when a solution is urgent.

My view? I don't feel much concern about what happens to my pets after they are dead. They have been disposed of by the Council, perhaps incinerated, perhaps buried on the tip, because both methods are in use locally. I believe that one cannot care enough while they are alive, and animals don't care after death. But this is a personal view and contrary opinions may be just as valid.

18 · Beaks, claws and nails

Beaks, claws, nails and hooves, all have the same basic structure. A sensitive inner core (the quick), surrounded by a dead, insensitive, keratinised covering which is the 'horny' nail, beak or whatever. The hard outside layer is continually replaced and continually worn away by abrasion on hard surfaces or materials. Dogs wear away their nails while walking on hard surfaces, birds wear away their beaks while chewing at bark, or gnawing at nuts. Well-behaved cats manicure themselves by scratching trees, and delinquent cats use a piece of well-polished pine or mahogany.

Life is easy for most house pets and there is not much wear and tear on their nails, which may elongate. It isn't that the nail grows too long, rather that it does not wear at a normal rate. Over-long nails can cause problems, but not as much agony as the average owner imagines.

Figure 1 shows a normal nail (it does not matter too much whether it belongs to a dog, cat, rabbit or tortoise). Cat's nails are retracted most of the time, and birds do not have a pad to walk upon, but all nails have the sensitive quick inside them and all nails have a natural length, below which they normally never wear.

Nails can over-grow and cause pain in either of two directions. Figure 2 shows a nail that has stopped wearing on its tip and started to curl round. If growth continues as it is, the point of the nail will penetrate the sensitive pad and allow infection to enter, just like a splinter in the foot. Each time the dog puts his foot on the ground the nail is driven into the senstive pad, and it must feel like walking with a tin tack penetrating through the sole of a shoe. Once the nail has begun to curl and its tip is no longer in contact with the ground, wear ceases and so, in effect, nail growth speeds up. This type of nail problem occurs in little dogs that are not heavy enough to hit the ground hard and wear the nail. Old and decrepit larger dogs might suffer in the same way if their walking is very restricted and confined to carpets or five minutes on the lawn. Such dogs have plenty of weight, sometimes so much that they are inactive, but the nails never meet anything that is even slightly abrasive so growth is never checked.

Figure 3 shows another type of over-growth. This usually happens in a flat-footed dog. the claws stick out nearly parallel to the ground and so the point does not wear. The nail lengthens because the dog is flat footed, and not the other way round. Long nails do not make the dog walk 'Back on

98

Fig. 1 A normal nail

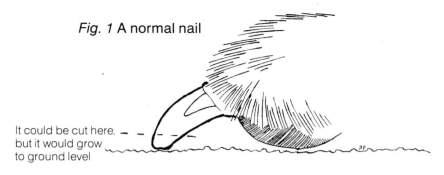

It could be cut here,
but it would grow
to ground level

Fig. 2 An in-growing nail

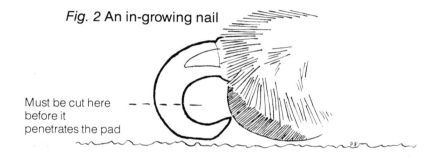

Must be cut here
before it
penetrates the pad

Fig. 3 An over-long nail

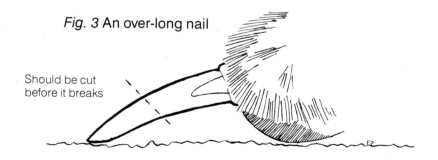

Should be cut
before it breaks

his heels', and cutting the nails will not alter the conformation of the feet. This over-growth is not painful, but it does increase the chance of breaking the nail. There is a 'pole vault' effect if the point of the nail hits the ground, and all the dog's weight falls on this thin column. Unlike the pole used by the athlete, the dog's nail has no elasticity and breaks under the strain. The sensitive quick is exposed and this can be very painful.

One might have a constantly over-growing nail if it has been broken at some time, or if some inherited deformity puts the toe in an odd position. The normal nails wear, the abnormal one does not.

Over-long nails and curling in-growing nails need cutting, normal nails do not. The majority of dogs and cats go from birth to a ripe old age without troubling a chiropodist at all. When nails have to be cut it is essential that they are cut properly. Giving a pedicure need not be done by an expert, but it is wise to start with some proper advice.

Should the nails be cut? The answer is yes if they are curling round, as in Figure 2, and if they are very long, as in 3. But a nail that looks like the one in Figure 1 does not need to be cut. Although there is space between the tip of the nail and the quick, and it would be possible to take a quarter of an inch off, that is no reason for cutting it. The tip of the nail is just in contact with the ground, it will wear at this length and remain at this length. If you cut a bit off the tip, it will grow until it reaches the length it is now – and then it will wear. Leave this type of nail alone, even if it makes a noise when it pitter patters on the lino – that's normal.

Is nail cutting a job for the expert? Not really, but whoever is doing it should know what he is trying to achieve – and have the right tools. If your pet needs his nails cutting at regular inervals it is quite reasonable to do this yourself. Ask your vet to show you how, and be prepared to spend quite a few pounds in buying a pair of nail shears. It is essential to use something that will cut cleanly. Ordinary scissors or very cheap nail shears twist the nail and may break it.

Where should the cut be made? It is essential to keep clear of the quick, and to leave at least a quarter of an inch between the quick and the cutting line. This is quite simple with white nails because the pink shadow of the sensitive tissue can be seen. When the nails are heavily pigmented and their black colour obliterates the quick, it is a matter of guessing where to cut. If some of the nails are white, they can be used as a guide – the black ones will be identical except for colour. All black nails present problems and the only thing to do is to err on the side of safety and leave them longer rather than make one bleed. It's sometimes possible to get an idea of the position of the quick by putting the nail shears in place, squeezing gently – not enough to cut – and watching the dog. If the pressure is on the sensitive area there will be some reaction.

Dew-claws are those part of the way up the legs, on the inside, the equivalent of our thumb. Just put the tips of your fingers on the table as you are reading this. Place the thumbs out sideways and this creates a digital diagram of the front legs of a dog or cat, four toes on the ground and a dew claw on each leg. Because dew-claws do not touch the ground during normal walking they are inclined to over-grow and may need cutting even though the other nails remain well worn.

Dew-claws are nearly always present on the front legs but occasionally on the back ones. It is usual to remove the hind dew-claws when the puppy is about three days old. The back dew-claws do cause problems; they will grow round in circles and penetrate the pad beneath and are easily and frequently broken. Front dew-claws can either be left on or removed. This is very much a matter of fashion. A dog without front dew-claws is less lethal to ladies' tights, but a properly trained dog that does not jump up uninvited, allows tights to reach their natural life span even if the dog is equipped with all his claws.

Dogs use the front dew-claws when climbing banks and galloping. Grass and mud are attached to the dew-claws of any dog when he's had a flat-out gallop on a well-mown field. Most reasonably active dogs manage to keep the dew-claw nails worn to a suitable length throughout their life, so they must be using them to some purpose.

Rabbits' nails, guinea-pigs' nails and any other mammal's nails work in exactly the same way. Rabbits in the average hutch have very little to wear their nails upon. A concrete block, or a couple of bricks provide an abrasive surface, as well as breaking up the flat expanse of a living hutch floor. Rabbits like to play games and 'King of the castle' keeps them occupied and wears the nails down. Guinea-pigs can do their own pedicure in a similar fashion, although a game as advanced as 'King of the castle' may be too exciting for a sober, phlegmatic cavy. Baby tortoises need sand-sheets (as for bird cages) to wear their claws upon.

Caged birds' nails may also become over-grown. When a bird has to sit on the same perch, day after day, week after week, his toes are always curled at the same angle and his nails always meet (or don't meet) the perch in the same position. In some cases the nails have no chance to wear at all and start to curl round because they never meet an abrasive surface. If there are four perches in a cage make certain that they are of four different diameters, with two of them round, one oval and one square. This will ensure that the claws grip in many different ways, the nails will wear and this toe exercise might help to prevent gout – a very common trouble of cage-living budgerigars.

Bird nail-cutting follows the same principles as any other nail, although catching can present problems in some of the large parrots. Perhaps catching itself is not too difficult, but a bad-tempered macaw is capable of cutting the catcher's nail, still attached to the finger. One method of overcoming this is to remove the perches from the cage and turn it on its side. The bird has to grasp the wires, and with a lot of patience it is possible to cut the nails as they protrude through the cage bars.

Beaks over-grow on some budgies. This is usually because of some very slight malalignment, and the upper beak does not wear as it should. Budgerigars strip the husk from their seed before eating it – which is why all that husk appears in the food hopper. Once a beak has over-grown, husking becomes very difficult and seed with the husk on is not very palatable or digestible. Extreme over-growth makes feeding impossible and a bird can starve to death.

Over-long beaks have to be cut and because the actual alignment of the beak is the reason for its failure to wear down, repeat cutting is usually essential. If a bird can be persuaded to gnaw at something hard he may wear his beak. Cuttle-fish and mineral blocks are the conventional beak wearers, but many birds ignore them or just use them as extra perches. Twigs of fruit trees can tempt a bored beak. All members of the parrot family are vandals at heart and enjoy nothing more than tearing anything to shreds. Apple or pear branches are non-poisonous, the bark strips off fairly

Cutting a budgerigar's beak

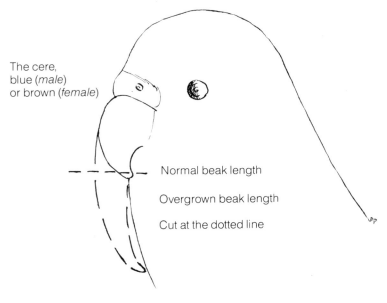

The cere, blue (*male*) or brown (*female*)

Normal beak length

Overgrown beak length

Cut at the dotted line

easily and the area around the cage looks like a logger's yard. But the beak has been in action and must have worn a little. Such branches help nails too because there is an infinite variety of diameters to grip. Collect such twigs from an unenthusiastic gardener, so that there is no possibility that he has sprayed his fruit trees with any insecticide.

Beak cutting can be a DIY operation in the same way that nail cutting may be. Good equipment and good instruction are the two prerequisites.

The incisor teeth of rodents and rabbits grow throughout life. (Dogs, cats and horses may appear to have longer teeth as they get older but this is simply because the gum recedes and more of the tooth is visible. It does not grow at all after it has fully erupted.) Those teeth that grow have to wear down otherwise they would extend to an impossible length. The top tooth grinds agaist the tooth in the bottom jaw and all is well – usually. Sometimes the teeth do not meet one another, so called mal-occlusion, which is not unusual in rabbits. When this happens the teeth continue to elongate and, if not attended to, will grow so long that the rabbit cannot close his mouth – and of course cannot feed. If one tooth is knocked out, the opposing one has nothing to wear against and grows to such an extent that feeding is impossible. Over-long teeth have to be cut at regular intervals. This is something that your vet should do, in the first intance at least. No pet enjoys tooth cutting but it is something that certain ones have to endure. Two minutes upset is preferable to starvation. Gnawing at hard wood or even stones will help to reduce the frequency of teeth cutting in some cases of mal-occlusion. I know of one rat that now has teeth of the correct length ever since he was given a large pebble encased in pastry twice a week. He wears his teeth while he is trying to get the last crumbs from the pebble. A new meaning to rock cakes.

All rodents need something to chew, otherwise they eat the plastic of their cages and may damage themselves on the sharp edges so produced. Branches from fruit trees and hard dog biscuits make safe and acceptable 'nibbles'.

19 · *Birds in cages*

Almost all birds are gregarious and many of the species kept as pets congregate in very large flocks in the wild. This instinct and desire for company of their own kind does not evaporate because they are living in our houses. So, my very first plea on behalf of caged birds is to keep two (or more). Bird company is important to birds.

I know that solitary birds are better talkers and more sociable birds than those kept in groups, but this behaviour is a reflection of their disatisfaction with their lot. Mimicry – expressed as talking – is the only way they know of attracting attention, and sociability can be an expression of utter loneliness.

It is not only caged birds that become humanised when kept on their own. Many years ago I had one duck, Quackers. She was brought to the surgery as a week-old duckling, unable to stand and with a tendency to perform backward somersaults – all the signs of vitamin B and/or E deficiency. She was given these two vitamins and made a miraculous recovery, but too late. The other ten ducklings in the clutch, plus mother hen that had hatched them, had been killed by a fox. Quackers' owner, a smallholder, was not interested in a duckling, and even less interested in any bill for the treatment that had saved this bird's life. It would have been money well spent if the other ten had avoided trouble, but the fee was more than one was worth.

So Quackers came home, and took possession of the garden. She decimated the slug population and was always delighted to see any visitor. As she became adult her delight extended to squatting in a position ready for mating whenever any human (of either sex) approached. Amusing behaviour perhaps, pathetic behaviour too, certainly indicating a need for company of almost any description. A friendly neighbouring farmer found a drake, Sir Francis, of course (what else could one call a drake?), and a beautiful friendship started at once. They were inseparable and humans had ceased to exist except as providers of food. If we went too close Sir Francis would defend his lady, and his peck, while hardly fatal, was a very sharp nip.

Quackers laid eggs which were, not surprisingly in view of the drake's constant attentions, very fertile and the farmer who supplied Sir Francis hatched a dozen ducklings every fortnight from them. Then Quackers suc-

Budgerigars can suffer from gout.
Provide different-sized perches for
them to exercise their toes. Mimicry is
one way of attracting attention.

cumbed to a fox. Within a week Sir Francis had changed character and looked to people for company. My youngest daughter was about two at the time and suffered considerably from Sir F's attempts at friendship. Her bottom was at duck-pecking height and the drake's attempts to chivy her into going slug hunting with him must have been very painful.

Quackers II, the product of one of Quackers' eggs, was introduced and, ignoring any incest taboo, Sir Francis became duck-orientated again. Humans were an interference, he had his own family.

Perhaps that is a long parable, but unlike many it is a true story and I think teaches us an important lesson about bird behaviour. They dote on their owner when they are very lonely. Contented birds tolerate people, but another bird is better.

Back to caged birds, and cages. Look for a cage to suit the occupant, rather than one that suits the rest of the furnishings in the room. Birds fly or hop in a horizontal, rather than a vertical, direction, and the tall, elegant bamboo cages, three times higher than they are wide, are totally unsuitable for any bird. Perhaps the best cage is the least attractive one, the 'breeder' cage, three solid sides and a wire front. Birds in such a cage have some privacy and protection from draughts, as well as space to move.

The positioning of the cage within a room can be important. Sunny windows are very nice if the birds can move away from the sun if they want to, but the window that lets in sunlight can let in cold during a winter night.

Birds have a very high basal metabolic rate. Everything works very quickly. The body temperature of a budgerigar or canary is about 107°F (dog is 101°, we are 98·4°). Breathing is rapid and the air passes through the lungs twice. It goes down the windpipe, into the lungs, then to air sacs in the abdomen. Then back through the lungs and out to the atmosphere. All this makes birds hypersensitive to strange vapours in the air. When something odd is about a wild bird will fly away, but the caged bird has to stay in his limited air space. Those of us of mature years remember when canaries were used to detect poor air quality in coal mines. If the canary in the cage survived, all was well, but if he died, danger was on its way, although miners could tolerate worse air quality than the bird.

There are dangers within modern houses from smokey atmospheres which upset caged birds, and some fumes are worse than others. Overheated non-stick pans produce lethal fumes, so be a careful cook if the bird lives within scenting distance.

All caged birds benefit from exercise and if it is at all possible they should be allowed and encouraged to fly free for some time each day. Bored birds, like bored people, eat to pass the time and obesity is the result.

It takes time to teach a bird to fly around the room, and even longer to

Birds fly in a horizontal direction, so avoid tall, elegant cages which are quite unsuitable. All caged birds benefit from exercise and should be allowed to fly free for some time each day. Indoor birds like a dampening too — it improves their plumage.

teach him to return to his cage when requested, although bribery with some selected food often works. It is a good idea to let a bird out for the first time inside a room when it is dark outside. This saves him from crashing against the windows and getting a headache. And darkness makes catching easier if he won't return to the cage; just switch off the electric light and he will perch where he was, waiting to be picked up. Whenever a bird is allowed out of his cage keep doors and windows closed and a fireguard in place. The updraught from a roaring fire can draw the bird into the chimney, and even when the hearth is cold it is no fun trying to extract a soot-covered bird from the chimney – and the bird doesn't enjoy it either. If a bird escapes through an open window it is not much use advertising 'answers to the name of Joey.' He won't when he's free, but many escaped birds are found when they perch on the outside wire of an aviary, showing us once again that birds like to be with birds.

Free flight has some effect on the decorations of the room. There may be extra spots of colour on the picture railing or the light shades. Budgies are chewers of everything, and the larger parrots even more so, thus wallpaper may be bitten and the electric flex can sometimes be at risk. Watch the birds, don't leave them too much to their own devices.

Parrots and mynah birds will create a messy area within a yard diameter of their cage. They flick food about, and throw sunflower husks and bits of fruit skin in every direction, so cage positioning is important with these larger birds.

Feather plucking is a recurrent problem. It is almost solely confined to solitary birds that have nothing else to do and they bite off their own feathers, sometimes to the extent that they are totally denuded of feathers – an 'oven-ready' appearance. If boredom appears to be the cause, then occupation is the solution. Green food to eat, bones to chew, dog biscuits to destroy are all helpful, but another bird to talk to is best of all. Don't put a second bird into the same cage. There will be warfare because, lonely though he be, every bird 'owns' his personal territory and does not welcome an invader. A useful trial of the benefits of company can often be arranged by bird sitting for a friend who is away from home. Put the two bird cages close to each other and see if feather plucking is reduced. The birds do not have to be of the same species for this trial to be worth while. If a feather-plucking parrot can squawk at a budgie or canary that is within sound and sight, he might forget his own feathers.

When birds are to be introduced to another, fighting will be very much reduced if they meet in a cage that is new to both of them. Neither 'owns' it and so neither needs to defend his territory. Make sure that this new cage has two water dishes and two seed hoppers so that the one that is second in the pecking order can drink and eat without being chased away. One of the least desirable characteristic of almost all species of birds is the way they treat each other. Although they enjoy company every bird bullies any other bird if he can get away with it.

Earlier, I talked about the atmosphere within our living rooms, in so far as fumes were concerned. Another difficulty is the very dry air in houses. Most birds in their natural state get caught in a shower now and again, and they don't always try to get out of the rain. Anyone who keeps budgies in an aviary outdoors has gone to investigate the noise when an April shower falls. The birds love it and stay out in the rain chattering and screeching, enjoying the feel of raindrops on their feathers.

Indoor birds like a dampening too – and it helps the plumage. When a new feather starts to grow it is enclosed in a sheath, rather like the wrapping around a magazine sent through the post. When everything is very dry, the feather sheath may fail to open, the young feather becomes stuck in a dried-up tube, and never develops properly. Some birds will use a bird bath, others never learn. A fine mist-spray of water each day helps the non-bather to develop better feathers. Use a hand spray such as is sold for misting house plants. There is no danger of a chill or any other upset. If you want to be extra cautious use warm water and spray early in the day so that the bird has dried off by bedtime, but that advice is to please nervous owners, it doesn't do much for the bird.

Nowadays it is possible to buy very good quality packeted seed and this is the simplest way to feed seed-eating birds. Enthusiasts with many dozen beaks to feed may make their own mixtures using canary seed, millet of various types and rape seed. I'm not sure that home-made is any better than the ready mixed, although it may be a bit cheaper because of bulk buying.

There is more to feeding birds than simply filling the hopper. Water of course is essential, so is a bit of flint grit, because these pieces of insoluble stone are the millstones of the gizzard and grind the food into a digestible texture. Dishes full of grit are not necessary. A budgerigar's gizzard is some-what smaller than a thumb nail and the grit-containing cavity in the centre is about the size of small pea, so very little grit is needed to fill it. Birds that are off-colour for any reason may eat abnormal amounts of grit if it is available – and an intestine full of stones does not encourage recovery. Bored birds might eat too much grit too, simply because they have nothing else to do.

Green food such as groundsel, chickweed, dandelion, lettuce, apple or seeding grass heads is an excellent extra for a caged bird. They enjoy the change and this non-nutritious food provides bulk and occupation without causing an increase in weight. Many birds in the parrot family eat and benefit from small amounts of animal protein. Parrots are not averse to a flake of fish or a chicken bone to gnaw. Some budgie breeders are convinced that their birds are helped to keep in tip-top condition by putting a chicken carcase in the aviary and allowing them to nibble the bits of flesh and fat still attached to the bones.

Mynah birds do not feed on seed alone. They are a close relative to our starlings which, as everyone who watches them knows, eat almost anything and vary their diet with the seasons. The starlings in my garden eat large amounts of elderberries in the late summer, and I drive a car with purple patches during August and September. Prepared food is available for mynahs, and this with fruit and perhaps a few mealworms now and again provides an adequate diet, but – one of the mynah disadvantages – profuse and semi-liquid droppings.

20 · Birds in aviaries

An outdoor aviary gives a bird much more freedom than a cage, and if the aviary is large enough, and properly furnished with perches and branches and private hide-away areas, birds can live in sizeable groups. Intelligent mixing is essential, and the compatibility of one species with another is something to find out from experienced aviculturists who have actually kept the birds in question.

Most birds are gregarious, and most birds are bullies. This may be an incongruous mixture of characteristics but ignoring it may lead to disaster in an aviary.

There must be several times more perching space than is needed – so every bird can find a place. Avoid small perches high up in the aviary. The top perch is always attractive and fought for. Shy birds need to be able to roost in a secluded spot, so arrange a solid barrier along one wall of the flight area or a bunch of twigs to break the sight line. Anything to give privacy.

A common fault in cages and aviaries is to site perches without thinking what is beneath. Sometimes a water or feed dish is placed directly underneath so that all the droppings go straight into the food or water. Other artistic arrangements of perches ensure that the bird on the lower row is constantly bombarded by that which falls from above. In fact he has enough sense not to stay there and this lower perch may as well not be there.

Several feeding and watering hoppers or troughs at various places around the aviary are much better than one central feeding and drinking point. Shy birds can feed undisturbed when there is an adequate choice of dining areas.

Provide adequate choice also when positioning nest boxes for breeding birds. Supply at least one more box than there are breeding pairs and place them all at the same height. It's not only human house hunters who look for the residence with the best view.

Any aviary must be escape-proof. A safety porch, so that one enters through two doors, both of which are never open at the same time, is almost essential. Failing that, the entrance door should be protected by a curtain or plastic strips so that birds cannot be tempted by an open space.

Foxes are a hazard in many urban areas. I lost twenty budgies from an aviary some ten years ago when a fox tore through half-inch mesh wire netting. Solid wooden sides, about two feet high around flight areas are safer when vermin are about. The enclosed part of an aviary must be substantial enough to be wind- and weather-proof. Remember that foxes can dig, so solid floors protect the indoor aviary, and a flagstone path around the outside of a flight area discourages mining activity. Ground-living birds, quail for example, may excavate large holes to use as dust baths. Flagstones on the inside perimeter restrict dusting to the centre space with less risk of an escape tunnel developing beneath the wire. If valuable birds are kept, human vermin are tempted and thefts are becoming more frequent. Locks that will keep birds in are not always good enough to keep thieves out.

21 · Birds that walk around the garden

Perhaps this chapter would have been better titled '... around PART of the garden' because large birds can be a disaster as far as the garden is concerned. Domestic fowl scratch and eat tender green shoots, diminutive bantams can denude a small grassy area in a very short time, ducks have webbed feet that can turn a lawn into a mudflat after a wet fortnight, and geese have even bigger feet so they only need one wet week to create havoc. Pheasants and peafowl can do as much damage as domestic poultry, but they are more likely to spread their wings and cultivate next door's garden as well – which does not make for continuing friendships. That's just the ornamental garden. Vegetable gardens suffer more because free-ranging birds get the first pick and damage more than they eat. If Muscovies get loose in May, 'duck and green peas' takes on a totally different meaning. The ducks really enjoy them.

These larger birds must be enclosed in some way or kept in such a large area that their depradations are hardly noticed. Earlier, I talked about Quackers and Sir Francis, without mentioning that they created a certain atmosphere – mud and worse around the back door – when they were waiting and asking, noisily, for food. They had nearly two acres of space to live in, so their damage was not obtrusive, because it was so diluted.

It is a matter of choice. Some, (many?) people might prefer to keep contented birds, and do not care if the garden suffers. Just decide beforehand which matters most.

Keeping poultry for egg laying can be an attractive proposition, except economically. Your eggs will cost more than they do in the supermarket, but you can be certain that, even if they are not true free-range eggs, they are laid by hens that have some freedom to walk about and scratch. In passing, anyone who objects to battery hens should keep their own poultry, if it is at all possible. There is no good method of keeping very large numbers of laying birds and if anyone is to make a living by producing eggs he needs to keep more than ten thousand layers. This number of birds on free range need a very considerable acreage of land and must be kept as many small flocks of a few hundred birds each. Even closing all the doors and opening them again next morning is a major undertaking, but if this is not done, foxes or mink can create havoc.

The main reason that very large flocks don't work is because of bullying, and those birds at the bottom of the pecking order have a very unhappy time for as long as they live – which may not be very long because their companions peck them to death. Not a nice thought but ignoring it does not change things.

I'm not enthusiastic about hens in battery cages, but it could be the least worse system when large numbers are kept, which is another reason for a few at the bottom of as many gardens as possible.

There is more to hen keeping than feeding and collecting eggs. They must have some indoor accommodation for roosting, laying and living in during bad weather. Free range must not mean without shelter at all times. There are few more miserable animals than a wet hen unprotected from an Easterly gale.

For six hens a shed six feet by four feet is about the minimum size. All the perches should be at the same height to prevent quarrels for the highest seat and six birds need three nest boxes – again at the same height and placed in the darkest corner of the hen house. Brightly lit nest boxes encourage vent pecking, which is what happens when one hen sees the bright-pink inside of the vent as an egg is being laid and pecks at this very sensitive part of her flock-mate. If the peck leads to bleeding the other birds will join in to the extent of disembowelling the victim. Hens can be very nasty to each other.

The outdoor run must be adequately fenced and properly drained. Unless they have many hundreds of square yards of scratching ground six hens will destroy all the grass in a very short time, and a smelly mess of bird droppings and mud is produced if the drainage is less than perfect.

Peat, forest bark or gravel spread at least six inches deep makes a much better surface than a trodden-down wilderness of bare earth. The peat or bark can finish up as useful manure in the garden, and gravel will last for several years, especially if it is hosed clean in dry weather.

The best birds for this type of environment are some of the heavier hybrids. Pure-bred poultry are relatively rare nowadays and most commercial flocks consist of hybrid strains, either white and lightweight – the 'leghorn' type (3–4 lbs weight) – or brown and heavier (up to 6 lbs), based on the Rhode Island Red. Larger birds are, in general, more placid, less likely to take off and fly over the wire or to fight and peck each other. At the end of the laying life a heavy bird makes an acceptable boiling fowl – if anyone can bear to eat Martha or Emily.

Hens lay the most eggs during their first two laying seasons. They start to lay at about twenty-two weeks of age and continue for fifty weeks. They then moult and start to lay again some six weeks later, for another year. After that the number of eggs drops considerably from perhaps 250 in the first year to below 180 in the third year. Egg-shell quality deteriorates as the bird gets older, and thin shells lead to broken eggs, sometimes as many as 20%.

Buying Point of Lay Pullets (advertised as P.O.L) is the best way to start a six hen enterprise, and if it is to continue they should be replaced at the end of their second laying season. This means they have to be killed, and competent humane killing is essential. It might be possible to find an experienced poultry keeper who will not only kill, but pluck and dress the bird. In any event I believe that anyone keeping poultry should be able to kill a bird that is injured or diseased and requires killing on humane grounds. Dislocation of the head from the neck is a most effective method, but like any other manual procedure it has to be learnt. Find a teacher, and if any bird dies, use this carcase to practise upon. Once you have done the deed on a bird that feels nothing, you will be much better able to destroy a suffering bird without adding to its pain. Of course your vet can destroy sick or injured birds by injection but this is not possible if an old hen is destined for the table. If Christmas chicken or turkey production sounds attractive, (naturally reared, no additives or hormones etc) don't forget that killing is necessary. I know this is not a pleasant subject, but ignoring it leads to inept destruction which no one can condone.

Proper feeding is essential if any reasonable quantity of eggs is to be expected, and food needs to be supplied in some reasonable type of feeding hopper. If this is placed outdoors the rain should not be able to fall in it, and wherever it is the birds should not be able to get into it or add their droppings to the food. Water containers should be such that they do not collect droppings or litter scattered when birds scratch.

Layers meal from a corn merchant or larger pet shop is essential, but don't buy too much at a time. Each bird will eat about 6 ounces per day, just over 2 lbs between the six. This food is packed in 56-lb bags (or the metric equivalent) and so one bag will last 28 days, which is as long as any food should be stored. Vitamins deteriorate and moulds can develop which reduce the feeding value of what was, when fresh, well-compounded food. In extreme cases stale and damaged food can be dangerous. Obviously this advice does not apply to canned dog and cat foods, but it is not wise to keep dog biscuits, hamster feed or bird seed for very long periods of time, and it is always sensible to keep food in vermin-proof containers. A dustbin, with a well-fitting lid, baffles most mice.

Household scraps can be fed, but egg production may suffer if they exceed 25% of the diet. Any waste containing meat products must be boiled for an hour before feeding. Waste vegetables, bread and cakes can be given without further cooking.

Grain and poultry pellets are conventional foods also, but I would not advise these for the half dozen birds that we are talking about. They can eat too much food too quickly, and having finished their feeding, birds look for something else to do. If they have been excited by scratching for corn that has been scattered in their run, the excitement may translate into pecking each other once the corn is eaten. Such mutilation is a major problem where birds are kept in partial confinement. Boredom starts it off, so anything that occupies them is helpful. Cabbage stalks can be pecked all day and peat or bark coverings on the ground encourage hopeful scratching (there might be a worm), but trodden-down mud stops any bird trying.

If cannibalism starts, act quickly. Clipping the upper beak square gives temporary relief, because this removes the point which causes further damage, but the basic reason – boredom – must be corrected.

An alternative to conventional poultry are bantams, miniatures of the domestic fowl and come in a great variety of breeds and colours. They are prolific layers of rather small eggs, but these are just the right size for rather small children. Bantams need everything that their larger cousins need, but on a smaller scale.

There is no need to keep a cockerel with laying poultry, either full-size or bantams. Of course his presence is essential if the eggs are for hatching – it takes two to tango and produce a fertile egg – but eating eggs need not be fertilised and in fact the vast majority sold for eating are from hens which have never seen a cock bird since they left the incubator.

Cock birds crow, and they crow at dawn, which, if you are a late riser, is at 4.30 am in the middle of summer. Thus they are not popular in urban areas. For every one who enjoys the cock's-crow, a dozen hate it. There will be neighbour troubles if a cock bird comes to live on any estate. Caponising (which is the bird-word for castration), stops a bird wanting to crow, but it is not permitted as a surgical operation, and chemical castration by the use of hormone implants is also prohibited as a result of EEC legislation. Dark chicken houses and low roofs, so that the cock bird cannot extend his neck, are two traditional ways of stopping crowing nuisance. They don't work. Unless you live in real country, don't keep a cockerel.

Turkeys, guinea-fowl and pea-fowl need the same type of feeding and care as domestic fowl, but rather more space – and they are all vocal birds. I suppose the best advice to anyone who wants to see peacocks strutting across his lawn, with tails displayed, is to suggest that he should buy a manor house and a hundred acres before getting the brds. Then his nearest neighbours will be out of earshot.

Waterfowl – ducks, geese and ornamental swans – need space and enjoy water. I believe that these birds have much more intelligence and sense of the ridiculous than any galliform (that's poultry, turkeys, pheasants, guinea-fowl and quail). Given the space they are delightful company in a large garden.

Domestic ducks (*above*) and geese (*below*) need space. Don't keep them in confined conditions.

Ducks need fox-proof night-sleeping quarters, and because they lay their eggs early in the morning are suitable pets for late risers. They should be kept shut in their sleeping quarters until at least 9 am in the summer, so that eggs are not scattered wherever the duck happens to be when she is seized by the urge to lay. Unless there is plenty of straw on the duck-house floor, eggs tend to be very dirty. Duck's don't bother overmuch about a nest, they just lay, but the right breeds, Khaki Campbells for example, will lay more eggs than a hen in any given time – and bigger ones too.

Ducks will thrive on poultry layers' mash and can tolerate rather more in the way of scraps and lesser-quality food. Given free range they will find considerable amounts of natural food for themselves during the summer months at least. Swimming water is not essential, but it is highly desirable, and breeding ducks need at least a large washing-up bowl to wallow in. Mating is easier and more effective when afloat and a sitting duck (on eggs I mean) will hatch rather more if she can go back to her nest, dripping wet, and so keep the egg shells moist and softer for the duckling to crack his way out of when the time comes. That's twenty-eight days for most and thirty-two to thirty-five for Muscovy ducks.

Geese are noisy and can be aggressive. Historians will remember that they saved Rome in 365 BC when it was attacked by the Gauls. They guard even more precious sites nowadays. A number of whisky bonds use these birds to mow the grass between the buildings in the day time and to act as mobile intruder alarms at night. Many geese pair for life and when a goose is sitting, guarded by her gander, it is a very brave person who interrupts this scene of domestic harmony.

Geese will eat large quantities of grass – four geese are said to eat as much as a sheep – and need little else in the summer months. When grazing is sparse some coarsely ground grain made into a mash plus boiled vegetables suffice.

Domestic ducks, geese and ornamental waterfowl need space. Don't be tempted by their undoubted attractiveness and keep them in confined conditions. They won't enjoy life, neither will you as the mud and mess builds up.

22 · Small, caged mammals

Small furry creatures in cages are often called 'children's pets', as if no one but children would be attracted to these animals. This is a total misconception, as anyone can find out by visiting one of the many rabbit, guinea-pig, rat, mice, hamster or other shows of small animals that are held in church halls and recreation centres throughout the country. Not only do a large number of adults enjoy exhibiting their pets, but I get the impression that most of the animals enjoy the day out and accept the extra attention as no more than their due.

But there is no doubt that most of these little things are kept as pets for children, even if father or grandfather gets mentally bitten and becomes an afficionado of the 'Fancy' – which seems to be a generic term for a group of people who have an interest in some particular species of animal.

Some pets are more suitable than others.

Rabbits are not the shy, gentle creatures that some story books imply. Large buck rabbits can be ferocious animals and it needs a stout-hearted adult to tackle them.

The smaller the better, and the dwarf breeds make more suitable pets for that reason alone. An adult weight of 3–4 lbs is manageable. Some of the long-eared white rabbits have been bred for meat production and will grow to 12–14 lbs weight by the time they are a year old. This is a very solid lump of rabbit, and weight for weight he will have a harder kick than any mule – with razor like claws at the end of the kicking leg. If this end fails, an angry buck rabbit bites, hard.

Does are smaller and gentler, but as with every species of animal, the 'good' pet is usually made so by a caring owner who starts handling and training early.

Two dwarf rabbits bought directly from their breeder are the best way of approaching this 'fancy'. Two does avoid breeding problems, but castration of buck rabbits is quite possible so one of each, or two castrated males, are other infertile combinations. I am quite certain that life is much happier for rabbits if two are kept together. There are thousands of solitary rabbits in hutches at the bottom of the garden, cold in winter, over-hot in summer. They are fed, except for the odd day when someone forgets, but if they have to endure this sort of life, it seems reasonable to allow them to do so in company. The winter nights would be warmer, and perhaps two rabbits would be remembered more often. These solitary rabbits are ill-chosen pets, and perhaps they would be a salutary lesson to potential pet owners – if only they could talk, or even scream.

Most rabbits live outdoors. They need a hutch that is wind- and water-proof. Many that are sold are too small, the timber is too thin, and there is no protection from driving wind or rain. Roofs should overhang so that the inside of the hutch stays dry wherever the rains comes from. It helps to place a sleeping box inside the hutch, so that rabbit can conserve his own body heat within a small area – a sort of double glazing that he can't see through.

Rabbits eat cereals or pellets mixed especially for them, and this is an-essential part of the diet. Almost every caged rabbit is under-exercised and too much concentrated food results in obesity and odd digestive disturb-ances. Natural rabbit digestion is based on fermentation of bulky food. They need fibre, even more than we do, and hay provides this for any caged rabbit – and he can spend time eating it without expanding his waist line too much. Supply the hay in a rack. Too many rabbits are given the same hay to sleep on or eat as they wish. They may have a simple choice between eating or freezing, and even when hay is in adequate supply who would want to eat, even edible, blankets after sleeping on them?

There are many myths about green food for rabbits. Listening to the horror stories about it causing diarrhoea, bloat, enteritis, (which is another word for diarrhoea, when used in this context but it sounds more frighten-ing), and tympany (ditto for bloat), one wonders how rabbits ever managed to populate Australia. There is a very simple answer. By the very nature of growing plants, wild animals' diets change slowly through the seasons. In mid winter, any food that is about, is dried up and very fibrous. As spring approaches green shoots appear, but in small quantities at first. Early sum-mer means that large quantities of succulent matter is there for the nibbling, life is very easy. Autumn starts with tougher food in large amounts, then back to winter scarcity. All gradual changes, and if we also make this gradual change of diet with our own caged rabbits (or guinea-pigs, sheep, goats or any other animal) digestive upsets will be very infrequent. Feast one day, famine the next, is a recipe for diarrhoea, wind and even the odd death.

Rabbits need water. Wild ones rarely drink during spring and summer. They get all the fluid they need in fresh greenery, but caged rabbits, living on dry food and hay have to top up with fluid from a water bottle.

Apart from feeding upsets the commonest rabbit disease is 'snuffles', a bacterial infection which tends to stay with a rabbit once he has met the germ. Sneezing, runny nose and general catarrh are the main signs. some-times the infection will spread to the middle ear and affect the balance, or

Rabbits are not the shy, gentle
creatures that some story books
imply. Caring owners start
handling and training their pets
early.

cause the rabbit to hold his head tilted to one side. Antibiotic treatment helps, but relapses are common.

Myxomatosis, which caused so many deaths in the wild-rabbit population in the 1950s, can affect domesticated rabbits, and it might be wise to vaccinate if the local wild population is affected. Rabbit fleas and a type of mosquito are the main vectors of this disease, so infection is possible even in a rabbit-proof garden. Wild rabbits have come to terms with myxomatosis to a large extent. The survivors from the 1950s appear to have been those strains that always lived above ground – and so mixed less and had fewer fleas. Their descendants follow the same life style and are that much less at risk. At the same time the myxomatosis virus appears to be becoming less virulent. Before the disease came to Europe it was well known in Colombia and very young rabbits were affected, showing swollen faces and feet, but most recovered. The virus that arrived in Europe was a more virulent strain and the European rabbits had no experience of such an infection, so no resistance, which is why they died in their millions. We are seeing evolution at work now. The rabbits best fitted to cope with myxomatosis survived and are breeding, while the virus may be reverting to a less virulent strain. Darwin would have been fascinated.

Rabbit claws and teeth cause some problems, and solutions are offered in Chapter 18.

Guinea-pigs are better children's pets than rabbits in my view. They are smaller, less self-opinionated, and seem content to sit about doing very little all day. I don't believe that they are even thinking as they sit – imagination does not appear to be their strong point. They have always been a domesticated animal and were house pets of the Incas – and also used as a food animal.

Even the mountains of South America are warmer than our chill damp winters and I would not ask a guinea-pig to spend the winter in an outdoor hutch unless it is wonderfully insulated, and the guinea pig has company and the very best of food. Even so, he may well need further indoor protection in the worst weather. Many guinea-pigs are taken indoors in bad weather but only get as far as the garage. Winter must seem very long, living in a dank, airless, dark cavern smelling of petrol and stale exhaust fumes.

The original guinea-pig evolved in an environment where plants grew every month of the year and green food was always available. By eating this fresh vegetation the guinea-pig obtained regular supplies of vitamin C, and so unlike many other animals never developed an ability to make this vitamin. We are not any cleverer in this respect but dogs, cats, rabbits, pigs and horses all manage to make their own supplies. A deficiency of vitamin C will cause the death of a guinea-pig and it is essential that the food

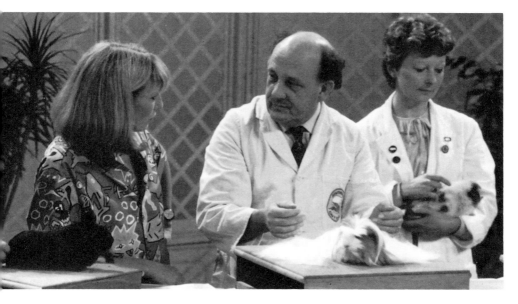

Guinea-pigs *(above)* are content to sit about doing very little — imagination is not one of their strong points. Hamsters *(below left)* need a metal cage — they eat wood and plastic. Glass 'gerbilariums' *(below right)* provide better accommodation than wire cages.

contains adequate amounts. Green food every day is sufficient, but it must be green. Carrot is not enough, although sprouted carrot tops will do. Apples are of little value but oranges contain plenty of the vitamin. There are vitamin supplements available in drop or tablet form and a Vitamin C tablet in the water bottle each day is one method of making a supply available, although there is a caveat here. Aluminium nozzles on the bottle will affect the vitamin and reduce its value. There are steel-nozzled water bottles available, and they are worth buying.

A standard small-mammal mixture, as for rabbits, provides the concentrated part of the food and once again good hay is a must. Good hay smells sweet, does not give out a cloud of dust when you shake it, and has a lot of the leaves of the grass still present. It's not all stalk. Be as fussy about your pet's food as you would when choosing the meat and veg for a special dinner party.

Nails and teeth cause problems, as already mentioned in Ch 18, and very many guinea-pigs are infected with a skin mite called Trixacarus. The mite can be present even though a very fit guinea-pig will not show any signs. If for any reason the animal becomes less than 100% fit, an intense itch, caused by the mite, results. If a female guinea-pig becomes pregnant, this extra strain can be enough to trigger off trouble, and her new-born offspring will begin life scratching. The irritation is often so intense that proper rest is impossible, feeding is interrupted by the need to scratch and the resulting weakness can lead to death.

Thorough shampooing with a suitable parasiticidal shampoo produces a rapid improvement, but continuing treatment is essential. Once the guinea-pig has finished each bath, the surplus shampoo can be well used to clean the hutch, and kill any mites that are hanging about, just waiting. Take scratching in a guinea-pig very seriously, and if you see your vet at the first itch, you can stop any serious upset developing.

Hamsters are popular, but I am not convinced that they make very good pets for children. Every time I say this I am taken to task and told about perfectly behaved ones that wake up each afternoon as if they know that school is over. I also hear about hamsters that sleep until 10 pm and then want attention, and about hamsters that bite.

Golden or Syrian hamsters are the ones usually kept and they are solitary animals. I don't know how many million Golden hamsters are kept as pets throughout the world but they are all descended from three youngsters that were found by a zoologist working in Syria. No others have ever been found as wild creatures – although escaped hamsters have set up homes for themselves in some places. Hamsters feed on the standard, mixed-cereal food that is made for rodents. They carry food in their cheek pouches so that they can store it for a rainy day – which should never arrive for a properly cared-for hamster. So if too much food is available, food stores are laid down in various parts of the cage, in corners and underneath bedding. They will eat fruit – but this soon goes off if too much is given. And beware of 'treats' such as sweets or chocolate, especially caramels, which can become stuck in the cheek pouches and set up infection there.

Hamsters need a metal cage – they eat wood and plastic – and regular cage cleaning is essential. Fortunately it is easier to move hamster food mountains than those larger ones made by the EEC.

There are other hamsters which are smaller in size, such as the Chinese and Russian hamsters. These are more gregarious and will live in groups.

Hamster exercise balls are on sale in some shops. This is a spherical plastic globe which divides into two halves. The hamster is placed inside the globe and 'walks' it about as he climbs the slippery inside. It is claimed that this allows exercise and the hamster is protected from the cat, and unable to go 'absent without leave'. I am not happy about their use for anything other than five minutes while the cage is cleaned out. Forced exercise of this nature (because the hamster cannot stay still if the ball is on a smooth floor) can lead to utter exhaustion and, although there are ventilation holes, heat stroke.

Gerbils came from Mongolia and are adapted to live in arid conditions. They drink very little water, and pass very little urine, which is a great advantage in a caged pet – no smell, little soiling of bedding. They will live as breeding groups if they are given enough space, although litters can appear every thirty days and there are six youngsters in the average litter – sometimes twelve. After six months, one pair of breeding gerbils creates its own housing problem. Two gerbils of the same sex will live together in harmony if they are introduced to each other when fairly young.

For feeding, use the standard rodent mix, but sometimes trouble occurs when the gerbils select sunflower seeds (those are the elongated striped ones) in preference to anything else. This odd diet is unbalanced and not conducive to good health and growth.

They drink little, but water should be available at all times, and especially for nursing females. Like all rodents they love to gnaw and while the standard wire cage is adequate housing, a large number of caged gerbils have sore noses because they damage them on the bars or by chewing plastic food containers. A 'gerbilarium' provides much better accommodation. This is no more than a glass fish tank, half filled with moist peat and straw, with a wire mesh top to keep the gerbils in and the cat out. They tunnel, they build mounds, and then they knock everything down and start again. Sheer enjoyment of living and being busy radiates from a gerbilarium. They need a food dish and water bottle of course, and twigs to gnaw upon add to the attractions. Because little urine is produced, thrice yearly cleaning and

Rats make the best small caged pets and feel at home with people. Furnish their cage (*below*) with a wooden climbing frame.

renewal of peat is about all the maintenance required. It may be necessary to dampen the peat occasionally, otherwise the tunnels collapse – but even that adds to the gerbils' fun.

Never handle gerbils by the tail – the skin can strip off. They are best restrained in a cupped hand, but they do move fast and it is as well to stay wide awake while holding a gerbil – otherwise he's gone.

Rats are, in my view the very best of the small caged pets. Most mothers are not keen on them, and grandmothers are inclined to remember that *their* grandmothers said that rats are dirty and cause disease. 'What about the plague?' they ask. Well, that was spread by the black rat and all the Fancy rats that are kept as pets are Norwegian ones, and the plague was at least 200 years ago.

Pet rats accept and enjoy being handled. They will curl up and sleep on a human lap, or shoulder, and they very rarely bite. During the first series of *Pets in Particular* we had some delightful rats in the studio. I was quite happy to allow two of them to wait up my sleeve while I talked about something else, and then allow them to appear in view when it was their turn. I would not have done this with a hamster, which might have bitten me, a gerbil, which would have escaped, or a mouse, which would have made me smell for the rest of the day. I have great faith in rats.

They can live in a large wire cage or an aquarium with a rat- and cat-proof top. It should be furnished with a climbing frame made of wooden rods or bars. For feeding, once again, use the standard rodent mixture. Rats will eat almost anything but too much meat or cheese can lead to a smelly rat. A mainly cereal diet avoids any of this.

Single-sex pairs will live contentedly together, and mass reproduction is not inevitable if more than one rat is kept.

Mice need the same type of care and housing as rats, but on a smaller scale. Whatever they are fed upon, there is a distinctive aroma about any room in which mice are kept. Cheese or meat makes the smell even worse but it's always there. They are very quick movers, which makes handling difficult. A mouse can be restrained by the tail, so long as his weight is supported by the cage bars or a solid surface. They should not be picked up by the tail only. Feeding is mainly cereal – the pet-shop mixture for rodents and a little green food can be used to give variety.

Like rats, mice come in many different colours and the Show enthusiasts are constantly breeding new varieties.

Chinchillas are somewhat exotic pets, and in a different price bracket to rabbits or guinea-pigs. £50 will buy you a fairly cheap chinchilla. They originate in the Andes and were once prized for their fur. A chinchilla coat was often more exclusive and more expensive than wild mink. Fashions change and almost all chinchillas in captivity are kept as pets or hobby animals.

They need a large cage, four cubic feet is about the minimum size for a pair, and shelves to sit upon and branches to climb upon are essential. They are shy creatures and a sleeping box is a must so that they can keep themselves warm and sleep secure in the knowledge that they are out of sight.

There are special chinchilla pellets for feeding, plus good quality hay and green food. They are very fond of sultanas and raisins – so much so that hand taming is not difficult once the chinchilla learns that the hand contains a sultana. Although hand taming is quite possible there are problems if chinchillas are allowed the freedom of a room. They will go anywhere, including up the chimney and under the settee. They won't go back to their cage, and they are almost uncatchable. However, they are nocturnal, so the only hope is that they will retire to the sleeping box at dawn.

Chinchillas love a dust bath of Fullers Earth, and they rotate in every direction at an extraordinary speed when performing this ablution. It is wise to put the dust bath into a larger box with high sides, otherwise the dust goes everywhere.

They need warmth – around 60°F as a minimum, so they must be kept indoors for most of the year. They are always sought after, so the babies produced from breeding pairs do not present any problems. There is always someone waiting.

Chipmonks are another less conventional cage pet. They are very fast movers too and any attempt to give them the freedom of the house is fraught with re-catching difficulties. If they are kept in a walk-in run it is possible to gain their confidence to the extent that they will take a flying leap and land on your shoulder (or head) and treat you as a part of the furniture.

There are many different species of chipmonks, and they are sometimes called ground squirrels. Basic care is the same as for any other rodents, but they are hyperactive, not only in movement but in chewing, so any wood that is part of the cage or exercise run should be regularly inspected to make sure that there is not a gap developing. This applies to floors too, they will tunnel in earth and eat a wooden one. A sleeping box must be part of the cage furnishings, and plenty of tree branches to gnaw and gallop round keep chipmonks happy.

If a breeding pair produces a number of offspring there should be an easy sale for these.

Feed the standard rodent mix, plus fruit and greens in regular quantities. Dog biscuits contain useful chipmonk food and they can get some of the gnawing out of their system while attacking a very hard biscuit.

Given the chance, all these small mammals breed readily. They know all about it, but their owner's always ask, so here is some basic information:

Species	Gestation	Eyes open	Take male away
Rabbit	30–35 days	9 days	Yes
Guinea-pig	62–70 days	At birth	May be
Hamster	18 days	7 days	Yes
Gerbil	24 days	21 days	No
Rat	22 days	14 days	May be
Mice	20 days	7 days	No
Chinchilla	105–115 days	At birth	No
Chipmonk	30 days	10 days	No

23 · *Fish*

In this chapter, and the next, I'll be talking about cold-blooded creatures, which have no fixed body temperature and whose activity varies according to the environmental temperature. The life of a cold-blooded creature is quite different from that of a warm-blooded bird or mammal, and when we come to fish, the fundamental difference here is that they live in water – all the time.

I am stating the obvious, but I wish that all fish keepers would realise the importance of water quality and temperature. Those three words 'all the time' are critical. Fish in a tank or small pond cannot get away to cleaner, warmer or colder water. They are trapped in their own little world.

When an unfortunate goldfish finds himself in the traditional spherical goldfish bowl he is incarcerated in a very small and utterly boring world. I do not credit fish with much in the way of imagination but I do sympathise with one that has to spend all his days swimming around in circles in an unfurnished bowl, and never seeing another fish to his life's end.

Traditional goldfish bowls are quite useful for protecting growing plants from draughts – African Violets thrive when their pot is placed in a fishbowl – but never use one for fish. The absolute minimum-sized tank should be 18 ins × 9 ins × 9 ins. This holds 5 gallons of water (if anyone wants to calculate the capacity of a tank, one cubic foot of water (6·25 gallons) weighs 62·5 lbs). Water is heavy stuff and a tank 3 feet long and 15 inches deep and wide, weighs nearly 300 lbs when it is full. You can't lift it and the weight on each of the four legs of the stand can make a hole in fragile floorboards.

But back to an acceptable tank. An inch or so of gravel should line the bottom so that water plants can grow in this. They help to maintain good water quality, add to the appearance of the tank and they provide some privacy for the fish. A rock, or even a plastic plant pot adds variety to the contour of the bottom of the tank and allows a fish to avoid light – or another unfriendly fish. This is the basic tank. Filters, aerators, and heaters for tropical and marine tanks are all extras and essential for certain fish, but for cold-water fish such as goldfish and shubunkins the basics will suffice.

One inch of fish per gallon of water (don't count the tail) is a reasonable housing density. The tank will not look very full, but the fish will benefit from the swimming and breathing space. Remember too that well-kept fish grow, and the two-inch tiddlers become six-inch monsters if they have a few years of the good life.

Some places within the house are better sites for a tank than others. Avoid bright window sills. These can be very cold on winter nights and the light will encourage the growth of green algae in the tank. This is no detriment to the fish, but when all the glass is stained green they are nearly invisible. Very dark corners do not help the plants to grow and brown algae can become a problem in low-light areas. And, I re-emphasise, do think of the weight if larger tanks are involved.

Over-feeding is the cardinal sin of kind-hearted, inexperienced fish keepers. Any food that is not eaten remains in the water and rots. One sees goldfish that are swimming in a thick cloud of fish-food soup because each day more flakes are added to thicken the liquid. It's not really true to say that one sees these fish. It's just possible to distinguish them in the murk.

Food-polluted water contains toxic breakdown products and rotting food uses up the oxygen in the water, so less is available for the fish. Caring people change the water, twice a week sometimes, and although this might make the tank look nicer total water changes are very stressful for the fish. If there is any variation in water temperature this causes as much shock to the (cold-blooded) fish as jumping from a hot bath into a pond of ice water would cause (warm-blooded) you. It is worse still if water is used straight from the tap. Not only is this at a much lower temperature than the tank water, but it contains a significant amount of chlorine. Any 'new' water must be allowed to stand for at least twenty-four hours before use, this allows the chlorine to disperse and temperatures to equalise.

If water changes involve handling the fish there is a further hazard. The scales may be damaged and this allows entry of any fungal spores that are hanging around – and they usually are. I suppose that there are more goldfish questions about 'fungus' than any other subject, and the most important part of any treatment is not what medicament to use, but what to do to get the fish into a healthy state when it is capable of overcoming fungus. And the very short answer to that question is good water quality, with a high oxygen content, and somewhat warmer than usual. At 65°F (reaching this temperature very slowly) fish eat more, grow faster, have a better and quicker circulation and repel infections more efficiently.

Avoid handling fish if at all possible. If a net has to be used make sure that it is wet and soft before putting it in the water. Dry, stiff nylon netting can be quite abrasive.

Tail and fin damage is often seen in fairground goldfish – those that survive their first week after being won – and this results from the unforgiveable practice of exhibiting fish in small polythene bags. There is very little water in these bags and the oxygen is soon used up. Under lights, the water heats up and a combination of stress and raised temperature causes the fish to wag his tail abnormally rapidly. Just watch the next time you visit a fair. The tail hits the polythene dozens of times each minute and each touch causes a bit of damage. Sooner or later the tail begins to die off, infection enters the injured tissues and someone wants to know how to treat tail or fin rot. The answer is the same as the Irishman gave when asked the way to Tipperary: 'Sure, I wouldn't start from here.' Don't start with fairground fish. They are not given any reasonable chance of survival. Don't try to win one; if you feel that they should not be there at all, and I do, then complain to the Local Council, the Environmental Health Department or the RSPCA Officer whenever you see fish offered as prizes.

I accept that fish are cold-blooded, that they do not have the same pain sensations as mammals, but I do not accept that even a less sentient living thing should be treated in this way.

Let's leave the worst and go to the best source of fish: a good, preferably specialist, pet shop or an enthusiastic amateur breeder of fish. Sometimes the latter develops into the former and I know several aquarist shops that are owned and run by former amateurs who ploughed their knowledge and enthusiasm into a business – and do it very well.

I condemned over-feeding, without defining it and saying how much food to give. Over-feeding means supplying more food than the fish can eat in ten minutes or so, and some is left and never eaten. The correct amount of food will vary very much, depending on the activity of the fish, warmer means more. Try a tiny pinch and wait and see. It is easier to give a bit more than to try to filter uneaten food from the water. Several small feeds each day are better than one feast. There is no doubt that fish get to know a feeding routine and can become quite excited at the approach of their food bearer. Many years ago one of my children kept two goldfish in a small tank in their bedroom and my wife used to give them an extra pinch of food at bed-making time each morning. These fish would almost flood the room by jumping and splashing on the surface in anticipation of their mid-morning snack.

These two fish were friends of everyone – everyone apart from a somewhat eccentric lady guest who was to spend a couple of nights in that bedroom. The lady asked for the fish to be removed because she 'couldn't possibly spend the night with livestock in the room'.

The same principles of fish keeping apply to outdoor ponds – but more so. There is a considerable amount of natural food in a living pond, so the fish can always feed without human help. In winter, feeding is rarely necessary, the fish are torpid and use very little energy because they do not move much, and unlike a warm-blooded animal they are not burning up food in

Traditional, spherical goldfish bowls are quite unsuitable for fish.

Several small feeds each day are better than one feast.

order to keep warm. Any garden pond should have a deep spot, with a depth of at least two feet so that a total freeze up is unlikely. If the pond is raised above ground level at all, a greater depth is necessary because there is no insulation from the surrounding soil Everyone knows (I hope) that ice should not be broken because there is a considerable shock to half-asleep fish when this is done. It is wise to melt a patch of ice if frost is prolonged. A tin full of boiling water placed on the ice is an effective hole borer, without upsetting the inhabitants.

Heat-waves cause more garden-pond problems, especially when humid thundery weather raises the water temperature. Any rotting vegetable matter in the water (lawn clippings for example) decays faster than ever and uses all available oxygen. And because there isn't a breath of wind, there are no tiny ripples which normally allow air to be absorbed into the water. The fish come to the surface, gasping, searching for that last little bit of oxygen. Use a hosepipe to create a fountain to splash into the pond and carry lots of oxygen in this sparkling water. Fish recovery is nothing short of miraculous when relief is given in time.

Lakes and slow-moving rivers can also have an oxygen deficiency when sewage or dead weeds decay at times of low-water levels and high temperatures. Although nothing is burning, gasping fish are delighted when the Fire Brigade turn up with their hose pipes. Goldfish and their various cousins breed well in any pond, the young fry survive in a well-weeded pond with areas of very shallow water. They can either hide amongst the weeds or bask in the warmer water that is only an inch or so deep. While they are hiding large fish have no hope of catching them – the cannibals would run aground.

Herons are a major enemy of fish in garden ponds and one of the incongruities of conservation is the protection of herons with no concern for the welfare of any fish. Netting across the pond defeats the predatory birds but looks untidy. A plastic heron is supposed to deter any real one from coming to feed because they are polite birds and do not disturb one another. This deception works for a time, but herons are not that stupid. Steep-sided ponds with a wall or fence at the water's edge are possibly the most heron-proof design. If the water is too deep to wade in and the poolside well above water level, the bird cannot perch in a fish-catching position. Where fish-catching cats are a problem, the anti-heron measures are equally effective.

Tropical fish come in all shapes and sizes. The temperature required varies a little from one species to another but water must be heated to between 70°F (22°C) and 80°F (27°C) for all tropicals. 74°F (24·5°C) is probably a good mean to aim at. Thus a heater is essential in any tank, and because things happen quicker at higher temperatures it is almost essential to have some type of aeration system. Plant growth speeds up at higher temperatures, but plants also need light so an overhead lamp that illuminates plants and fish is both decorative and practically helpful.

Not all species of fish live in perfect harmony. Some eat their own species, given the chance, and many eat other species. Some just fight because they are aggressive by nature. Find out from someone well experienced – a member of an aquarist society, or a trusted fish supplier – before filling a tank with fish chosen simply because you like the look of them. It's much more important to find out if the fish like the look of each other.

Tropical fish grow more rapidly than cold-water fish and so over-crowding can happen in a shorter time. Many popular species breed easily, and in a well-planted tank quite a number of the youngsters will be able to hide amongst the weeds until they are too big to be a tasty morsel for a larger fellow fish. Over-population soon occurs, which is another reason for starting with a very few fish in quite a large tank.

Marine fish are the most demanding of all. They are also the most spectacular in terms of colour, shape and activity. Water quality is absolutely vital where these fish are concerned and quite small deviations from the correct salinity can lead to disaster. Learn all about fish keeping first before you start on marines. They are expensive, almost all are imported and after that very long journey they deserve to be well kept.

24 · Snakes, lizards, tortoises and others

There are many cold-blooded animals that live on land, and some that spend their time commuting between land and water. A few of the many thousands that fall into this category are kept as pets, or more precisely as hobby animals. When a devoted enthusiast is in charge all goes well and the major difficulty is increasing the size of the accommodation as the snake, lizard, iguana or terrapin grows. And if they are well kept they grow very rapidly. Temperature is critical and low temperatures slow things down and a decline sets in, so one piece of advice to any reptile keeper might be, 'If in doubt, raise the temperature if it is below 80° F (27° C).'

Most reptiles and terrapins are kept in a glass tank, known as a vivarium. This is basically an aquarium without the water, although some snakes like a pond in a corner of their vivarium, and terrapins are usually given three quarters of their living space as a pond and only a quarter as dry land for a basking area.

Non-venomous snakes are the ones usually kept as pets. There are people who keep rattlesnakes and cobra but only if they hold a licence under the Dangerous Wild Animals Act, which should impose stringent conditions not only for the well being of the snake but also for security so that anyone living nearby is not likely to be in urgent need of anti-venom after a bite from an escapee.

I do not recommend anyone to keep snakes of any description, unless that person has a serious interest and enough money to provide better than the minimum care and living conditions. There are often adverts offering five-feet long pythons or boa constrictors at prices of around £50. A worrying number of these are bought as conversation pieces. 'Come and see my snake,' can be a modern alternative to viewing etchings.

If, after all that, a snake is still on the shopping list the minimum housing should be a vivarium, at least half as long again as the snake, which means a very large tank for a five-foot boa. It must be heated to about 78° F (25° C) and the heater is best placed at one end of the tank so that there is a temperature gradient and the snake has the choice of a hot or cooler spot.

Many snakes like to lie along a tree branch or on a large rock, so these should be part of the furnishing of the vivarium. Gravel can cover the floor. The top must be escape proof. If a snake has nothing to do and is feeling active he will try to get out, and it needs a very small aperture to make this possible. I know, and you know, that a relatively small python is no great danger to anyone living nearby, but they don't believe this. For the neighbour's sake as well as the snake's make sure that he stays in the warm where he is intended to be. If the top of the vivarium is solid material, and if a rim of black paint is put around the top three inches of the glass, there is much less incentive to try to push out, and less danger of such pushing damaging the scales around the snake's head.

Small snakes are fed on a basic diet of mealworms, but they do need other types of food to remain healthy. Dead mice, rats, and day-old chickens are essential extras. Chickens are the easiest to obtain. Cockerel chickens of the egg-laying strains are of no possible commercial value. They grow up into very skinny, long-legged carcases that no one would want to eat. Thus they are killed as soon as they are hatched and it is possible to buy these chicken carcases deep frozen. They provide a valuable food for snakes, captive birds of prey, owls and some of the small carnivorous mammals. Perhaps this is not a pleasant subject to read about, but if we take responsibility for keeping any captive animal it must be properly fed. Don't keep them if you don't like the thought of what they eat. It is not essential to feed live animals to snakes and I do not believe that this should ever be done. They can be trained to take carcases so long as they are warmed to blood heat.

Many species of lizards are on sale. Each has its own particular food requirement. Many will eat maggots and the bluebottles that hatch from them, while others are satisfied with slugs, worms and mealworms. A vivarium heated to at least 70°F (22°C) is essential for the warm-living lizards and they enjoy bright light, so an electric light bulb shining on one end of the tank gives them a basking area which they can imagine is under the sun.

Chelonians is a collective name for terrapins and tortoises, perhaps the two commonest cold-blooded pets after fish. Since January 1984, the importation of tortoises has been prohibited except for those destined for reputable zoological collections. In the past, perhaps 80% of those that were brought into this country died within a year, and the trade was such that tortoises have become rarities in some of their native habitats.

One result of this ban on imports has been an enormous increase in the price of a tortoise. Up to £150 is being paid and reports of tortoise rustling have appeared. The shortage has certainly increased the interest in good husbandry of tortoises and now 'they've never had it so good'.

Tortoises need warmth (around 65–70°F (18–21°C)) when they are awake, and cool conditions (perhaps 40°F (4°C)) when they are hibernating. Anything in between is very bad news for a tortoise; he is awake and semi-mobile, but not alert enough to feed. He uses energy in his slow-moving wanderings and does not replace it.

Nature did not intend that they should have to cope with British weather.

Depending on the particular species, in warmer climates they hibernate for two to three months, but here sleep for six months and wake up in April. They do not then recite Browning, 'Oh to be in England, now that April's here.' If a tortoise comes out of hibernation and does not start to eat and drink within a day or so, warm him. If it's too cold outside he will have to stay in a heated pen indoors. A circle of hardboard will restrain him, a polythene sheet will protect the floor, and newspaper is a suitable temporary floor covering on top of the slippery polythene. Dependent on the house, green house or out-house temperature, the tortoise circle can be heated by an electric light bulb suspended above it, an electric fire (out of tortoise range) or any other means that an ingenious owner can devise. Just make sure you reach 70°F (21°C) somehow.

A very effective warm-up is provided by a warm bath. Place the tortoise in a bowl of water, just below blood heat (ours) for about twenty minutes. Keep his head above water, of course, but a splash around the mouth and eyes does no harm and might encourage him to drink. They are dehydrated after six months without a drop, but then so would you be.

If the tortoise passes a motion during these ministrations it is a sign that activity is returning and that bowel movements are beginning. And because the tortoise is a fairly simply designed animal, emptying one end is a stimulus to start feeding to fill the other.

Try feeding with lettuce, tomato, cucumber, cabbage, french or kidney beans, and sweet alyssum (yes, the one with white flowers that is used for summer bedding. I had a tortoise which used to clear any flower bed of this particular plant. I *know* this one is safe but beware of others).

Every tortoise has a different palate and they are very decisive about food choice. One thing is quite certain; even in mid summer, lawn grass alone is not enough. With another six-month sleep looming ahead every tortoise has to stuff as much food into himself as possible in (what is to him) the very short summer.

They are not exclusively vegetarian and enjoy the odd spoonful of canned cat-food. Find out what your tortoise likes and indulge him.

Like any other animal, tortoises enjoy the company of their own kind. There are two common species: Hermans tortoise, which has a horny hook on the end of its tail; and the spur-thighed tortoise, which (surprise, surprise) has spurs on the inside of each hind leg, either side of the tail. Male tortoises have a longer tail and usually the shell on the base is concave.

Given a pair, eggs may well be produced. Male tortoises are enthusiastic sires and courting behaviour is noisy. He approaches her, sideways on, at full speed and pulls his head in just before the collision. One wonders who has the headache.

If eggs do arrive it is possible to hatch them, but don't undertake tortoise breeding unless you are prepared for a long period of devoted attention to the young tortoises. Long is a couple of years. Incubate the eggs in a box of dry sand at a temperature of 86°F (30°C). An airing cupboard might be warm enough; a heated seed raising tray can suffice or even an electric light bulb suspended over a tray of sand might give enough heat. Use a thermometer to check. Incubation time varies with temperature but is between two to four months. The sex of the young tortoises varies with temperature also: over 86°F results in mainly females; below 86°F, mainly males.

Once the eggs are hatched the work begins. The shell is soft at first but hardens within a day or so. They need a wash to remove surplus sand as soon as they emerge. Feeding starts from the first day. Green food such as cabbage, cress or lettuce; fruit such as apples, plums or soaked raisins; and either cat food, chopped spratts or chopped-up day-old chicks. They must have enough calcium and phosphorus to develop bones and the growing shell, and a whole carcase of fish or chicken will provide this, otherwise some supplement is needed. Crushed baked egg shells will supply calcium, and halibut liver oil will supply Vitamin A and D. Stick a pin in a capsule of this oil and put a drop on each youngster's food.

They need heat of course – a generous 70°F (21°C) is the minimum. Sand sheets, as made for the bottom of bird cages, should be used over part of their floor area so that the claws can be kept worn down. Watch for youngsters stuck on their backs, they are inveterate climbers and fall upside down. This applies to adults too, especially if there is a rockery in the garden. No matter how often a tortoise lands on his back he never seems to get put off.

Tortoises do not *need* to hibernate. Youngsters develop faster if they are kept warm during their first two winters and continue to feed. Adults that have had a poor summer, eaten little and do not look fat (inspect the inside of the thighs and armpits – a tortoise expands there, not around his waist) have a better chance of survival if they are kept warm and feeding all winter. Since the banning of tortoise imports there have been some American Box turtles offered for sale as a substitute. They are completely different. The box part of the name refers to the underneath shell which is hinged, so the turtle can shut himself up in his box when he feels that danger threatens. They need more heat than tortoises, and are mainly carnivorous when young and omnivorous when adult. They don't hibernate either. So don't be persuaded to buy a 'near' tortoise unless you know more about it.

Terrapins are the other popular chelonian, and while they come in many varieties the red-eared one is the one that arrives in its tens of thousands for sale in pet shops. They are usually sold when very young and small. Like all young things they are active and attractive. They grow, quite quickly into large, less active and not quite so attractive adults. The photograph on page 141 shows a tiny 2-inch diameter youngster and an adult, of about four or five years older and seven or eight inches long.

For two young terrapins a tank 2 ft × 1 ft × 1 ft is just about sufficient, but won't be for long. At least a quarter of the tank should be filled with dry gravel or rock, and if an electric light bulb is suspended over the beach the terrapins can sunbathe and allow their shells to dry out. In such a small tank the light bulb may supply sufficient heating, but a thermometer should confirm this – guessing is not good enough. Aim for 75° F (23° C).

Terrapins *cannot* be kept without some artificial heat. I have heard of 'cowboy' pet-shop operators suggesting that the addition of half a pint of warm water to the vivarium each day is enough to keep them warm. This is utterly irresponsible advice and absolute rubbish.

Feeding is on shrimps, chopped herring, sprats, earthworms or proprietary terrapin food. They will eat pieces of raw meat or liver. Terrapins always feed in water and prefer to tear their food apart before eating it. This means that the water is soon contaminated with flakes of meat and remains of fish, so frequent filtration or a change of water may be needed to keep the tank in an acceptable condition. One way round the dirty water problem is to remove the terrapins into a large bowl of water (at exactly the same temperature as the tank water) and let them feed in this bowl. Then the messy water can be disposed of after each meal.

Imported terrapins may harbour various salmonellae, a bacteria which can cause food poisoning in humans, so 'now wash your hands' applies particularly to terrapin handling, and it's a good habit to get into after touching or stroking any animal.

Apart from cold conditions causing lethargy and failure to feed, there are two deficiencies that account for nearly all the terrapin troubles. Calcium deficiency leads to soft shells, and Vitamin A deficiency causes an eye trouble characterised by swollen eyeballs, which can lead to blindness. Both are easily cured, and better still prevented by feeding some halibut liver oil – from the capsule as described for baby tortoises – and either crushed baked egg shells or bone meal as an extra in the diet. As much bone meal as will sit on the side of a match stick is enough for one terrapin. Use the brand sold for feeding, not the brands that are sold for the garden. A dog breeder or your vet might be able to supply the few ounces that a terrapin needs. Bone meal tends to be available in 2·5-kilo sacks only.

Given this basic attention, terrapins grow and will need a mini-pond, so decide, before buying the little ones, if you are prepared to house them till death you do part. Terrapins live a long time and I know several pet shops that have taken pity on large terrapins that have outgrown their tank and are willing to give them to anyone who cares enough. No one seems to.

Terrapins have quite a bite so beware when hand feeding, and never keep them with fish – they may eat them.

'My, how you've grown!'

(Below) Some iguanas are partial to a piece of banana.

25 · *A bit about ponies*

And a 'bit' is all it is going to be. There are dozens, perhaps hundreds, of books about good horse keeping, stable management, and how to care for your pony, and yet there are still too many ill-kept, miserable, bored ponies waiting patiently in fields around all the big cities. In many suburban areas the few farms that are left have abandoned agriculture in favour of horsey-culture.

The economics of pony keeping are very similar to those of running an old motor car. Pony or car can be bought for between £200 and £400, and either might be described as a 'good runner'. But the costs of running are much more than the purchase price.

A pony must have somewhere to live, and just sharing a field with other horses will cost £5 or more per week. PONIES DO NOT LIVE BY GRASS ALONE, unless they are in a very favoured part of the country, have an extensive acreage to roam over and are not expected to work. However we have reached £250 per year. Some extra food will be needed. Hay for twenty weeks at £2·50 per bale (one bale a week) costs £50. A few pony nuts for the worst of the winter and the hardest working times in the summer could cost another £25. Ponies need shoeing and their feet trimming, REGULARLY, six visits by the farrier each year, sometimes just to cut the feet, sometimes to fit new shoes, will cost £80 or so. Then there are veterinary fees, which include flu and tetanus boosters – ponies are not allowed on any racecourse where gymkhanas or similar events might be held unless they have a 'passport', identifying the horse and certifying that the flu vaccinations are up to date. If any working pony gets through a year without needing at least one other veterinary visit, it is a very fit, and lucky pony. And don't forget worming. Let's allow £50 for all that. The total has now reached £455, and any repairs to tack (that's the saddle, bridle, head collar and all the other necessary pieces of equipment that are essential to good riding and horse keeping), insurance of horse and rider, entry for and transport to horse events are extras. If the field is a distance away from home there is daily transport – and better still twice daily, to see that all is well and to convince your pony that you still care.

In cash terms, £500 per year may not be enough.

Time costs are heavy too. Any living animal, with the possible exception of cold-water fish and hibernating tortoises, should be seen at least once, and much better twice, per day. Seeing a pony does not consist of looking out of a steamed-up car window on the way to school and being satisfied if he is still standing on his feet. Go into the field – even if it's muddy – and take a piece of bread or a few pony nuts at every visit. If he comes to expect a tit bit he'll trot across the field to meet you, which means that any stiffness or lameness shows up, and if this routine welcome does not occur it is a warning sign that something is very wrong. Then talk to the pony, if he's having hay and sharing the field, make certain that he's getting his share. Stay with him while he is feeding. When half a dozen ponies are gathered together there is always one unfortunate that is pushed away from everything – including the hay rack.

I hope I have convinced someone, somewhere, that £500 per year would buy a lot of hours of riding at a good riding school. Anyone who is such a valuable client will almost certainly be able to ride their favourite pony every time. Not quite as satisfactory as ownership for the rider perhaps, but the pony is looked after by someone who is single-mindedly caring for horses, which may be much better for the four-legged part of the partnership.

But where my arguments have failed and someone is about to buy their first pony, and parents have been brainwashed to believe that he will be well-cared for each and every day, and Mum will not have to take over, here are a few suggestions.

Buy a pony that you know. Perhaps from the school that has taught you to ride. Perhaps your favourite pony. There is no such thing as a perfect horse, but there are suitable ones, and those that are less trouble than others. It's worth knowing that a pony is easy to catch. A morning's riding loses its attractiveness if it does not start until noon, because the past three hours have been spent chasing a pony around a field. What is even worse is that the pony shows every sign of having enjoyed it. He should be easy to box and shoe. And (to parents), that pony should know more about riding than your son, or more likely, daughter. A mature, not to say elderly, pony has seen it all before, nothing surprises him. He's shock-proof, nearly bomb-proof. Steady enough to be in charge of your child.

Such a paragon of horseflesh might not be a show winner, or have little hope of wearing a rosette in high-class company. He can compete in less major events and he can cultivate that bond between horse and rider which is the basis of all good horsemanship, but which never develops unless the rider has complete confidence. The old schoolmaster pony will develop confidence in a way that a young horse could never do.

Just like shoes, a child's pony should be the correct size when first used. It is foolish to buy one (or two in the case of shoes) that will be the right size in a couple of years. The ground looks a long way beneath when anyone is sitting in a saddle for the first few times – even when mounted on the right sized horse. If a six-year old is put on a pony that suits a twelve-year old, the height above ground must appear enormous and cannot help anyone's confidence.

Most parents want their children back from a ride undamaged (I know there are times when you never want to see them again, but that wish does not last long). Well-fitting hard hats are essential, complete with chin strap that keeps the hat firmly fixed. And, in passing, if you find a riding school that is not paranoic about protective head gear, choose somewhere else to ride.

Second, third and subsequent ponies may be of a better class, in the performance or competition sense. If so they will be much more expensive and cost nearly as many thousands of pounds as the first pony cost hundreds. Again try to buy a pony that you know. Adverts are masterpieces of superlatives and the fact that a pony comes from a long way away does not make him that much better. It may mean that he's too well-known in his own district for anyone to want to buy him. When considerable sums of money are involved, it is well worth having a veterinary examination before purchasing any horse (or any other animal for that matter). It used to be known as a 'soundness' examination, but because absolute perfection does not occur in this world, and because lawyers can suggest that any tiny departure from perfection means unsoundness, that conception has been abandoned and substituted for a certificate of suitability – a much more sensible concept. A child's first pony could be perfectly fit, free from every blemish, utterly 'sound' in the old way, but if that pony was a very bad-tempered stallion inclined to bite anyone and kick those he could not bite he would hardly be suitable as a child's riding pony. A phlegmatic old horse with the odd lump on his legs, might not be 'sound', but could be the most suitable animal possible.

Let's finish by talking about some delightful miniature horses that we saw in the last *Pets in Particular* – Falabella horses, true miniature horses. Horses are usually measured in hands – which is four inches – and the height is taken from the withers, the top of the hump in the spine just above the front legs. A small pony is eleven or twelve hands and a very big horse is just over seventeen hands. Falabellas are measured in inches, and thirty-four inches is the maximum height.

They originated at Senor Falabella's ranch in Argentina where one miniature stallion was discovered, living wild. Selective breeding for generations has produced today's perfectly proportioned tinies. There are some differences between Falabellas and the more conventional horses. These small ones have a month's longer gestation period – almost thirteen months compared to around 340 days in most mares. Less surprisingly, they have two less ribs and two less vertebrae.

Buy a pony to fit the child.

Miniature horses are delightful, but too small for riding, and very expensive.

The foals are very tiny, about sixteen inches high, and it is no trouble to nurse one on your lap – although I'm not sure that the foal appreciates this attention.

Too small for riding, they are real 'hobby' animals, although the hobbyist has to have a deep pocket because Falabella horses cost around £4000 each, and, as ever, one by itself would be very lonely.

Very few people will ever keep them, but we can all admire and wonder at this perfection in miniature.

26 · Moving house, mixing pets and cat flaps

Change is part of life, but that does not mean it is always enjoyable, and while we can look forward to some alterations and tolerate others most animals resent change. They like life to continue as it ever was.

Moving house cause difficulties for certain pets. Those in cages don't mind, in fact the house has not changed. Most dogs accept it because their owner, the pack leader, is still there. However, a change of home is a traumatic experience for many cats. The greatest difficulties arise with the shortest moves. Cats have quite a large territory, which may consist of a small area – their own garden perhaps, of which they are in sole possession – and a much larger area through which they wander during the day or night and which is well mapped in their subconscious. So a move of half a mile does not take the cat out of his familiar surroundings, which may extend to a couple of miles or more. You have moved, so has the furniture but the cat's internal map is unchanged. This is the cat that constantly returns to his old home simply because memory takes him there.

A solution to this short distance difficulty is to board the cat for a month immediately after moving. This allows his memories to fade and he is more likely to remember his first meal in his new home after a month in kennels and returns to the right place for subsequent feeds. Three- or four-mile moves may be made easier by taking the cat on a circuitous journey between old and new houses. They have a homing ability – not up to pigeon standard, but it's there nevertheless – and many twists and turns may confuse this memory so that the way home is forgotten.

Cats have a problem with their exclusive territory when they move. The garden of your new house has passed into your ownership with the deeds or the tenancy, but no one has told the cat next door, and the flower beds and lawn have always belonged to him since he was a kitten. So he fights to retain what he owns when he finds that a new cat has arrived on the scene. I've talked about abscesses earlier and moving can lead to them, but the cats have to sort it out between themselves. They often become good friends and allies, well able to knock the stuffing out of any third-party cat that dares to cross the boundary.

Many movers worry about how the cat will travel, should he be tranquillised? My answer is a categorical NO. A cat needs to be in full possession of every one of his faculties when he arrives in a strange house. He is much better off if he has all his strength and sense while travelling. A semi-comatose cat does not have enough sense to find the warmest (or coldest, depending on the time of year) corner of the basket, or to brace himself if there are any jolts or bumps during the journey. He may not like it, he may give voice to his unhappiness, but a four-, six- or even twelve-hour journey for one day in his life is not exactly un-endurable agony. It's just unusual and a bit unpleasant.

A proper travelling basket is essential. DIY cardboard boxes don't always work and if the cat nips out when you stop at a service station he is lost because very few cats carry a map of the motorway network in their head.

There are nearly as many opinions about how to treat a cat when he gets to his new home as there are cats. I am in favour of allowing him out to explore his new surroundings as soon as possible. Wait until the removal men have left and calm has descended, even if the chaos of packing-cases remains. Wait until the cat is hungry and it is a couple of hours past feeding time. Then let him out and after five minutes the sound of a tin opener or the clatter of his dish should bring a hungry cat back at a gallop. Continue this routine for ten days or so and he will have mapped out the immediate environs.

A toilet tray *outdoors*, placed inside a tea-chest laid on its side, can be a great relief to a cat in unfamiliar surroundings. The tea-chest stops the litter becoming wet and soggy, but it also gives the cat a sense of security while he is busy concentrating on his tray. There is no danger of an unfriendly cat pouncing on him while he is at a disadvantage. If a toilet tray is placed indoors there may be difficulties in the future in re-training the cat to use outdoors again.

Cats move best in cold wet weather when there is no encouragement to wander and the resident cats, already in possession, stay indoors. Dogs should be controlled and come when called so that straying should not be a moving-house hazard. A dog does need a new disc on his collar *before* he changes house. Make extra certain that booster injections are up to date too. Living in a new district might mean that he meets slightly different varieties of the various dog infections, and an extra boost to his protection can do no harm and might prevent trouble now and again.

Fish, in any quantity, present moving difficulties. The tank in the new house should be established before the fish are put into it, but this takes time and assumes that there is somewhere for the fish to swim while their tank is being transported. This is where membership of an aquarist society can be very useful.

Garden pond fish are best left with the pond and house. They are established in water that they know and don't deserve any disturbance.

Mixing pets causes a lot of worry and heart-searching to owners. More than it does to the pets in many instances. Of course any well-established animal resents an intruder in 'his' territory. Time is a great healer, and the result of most mixings of animals is a solid friendship. Love at first sight is not all that common between emotional humans. Sensible animals eschew such an instant decision.

Whenever animals live together there is a social order. One is top dog, one remains downtrodden and inferior to all the rest. The pets sort themselves out, we cannot influence the order of precedence and any attempt to interfere usually cause more spits and snarls than they ever prevent. Let animals meet for the first time where any one of them can retreat, with dignity. If a cat meets a new kitten in well-furnished room (plenty of furniture I mean, not high quality), the kitten can hide behind an easy chair and the cat does not have to fight to assert himself. He can pretend that kitten is not there. When cat meets a new puppy, the cat can always get out of the way by hopping onto a chair. Let them see each other from different altitudes, then each is safe. But what about the puppies eyes? There is a possible risk of their being scratched in pop-eyed dogs such as pekes or pugs, but most pups eyes are scratched when either the cat or the puppy is being restrained by a good-intentioned owner interfering. Left alone, pup would have dodged, or the cat would have been able to walk away.

Birds in cages and little furry pets in hutches accept a newcomer if they can meet in an unfamiliar cage, that belongs to neither. No one has any territory to defend.

Sight barriers help a rabbit or guinea-pig to settle down with a fresh companion. A brick or large log in the middle of the run allows one to sit one side and one the other. They do not have to accept a challenge if something solid is in the way. A thick bunch of twigs can form an equally effective barrier to help fresh birds in an aviary.

Food is a potent cause of quarrels, so feed new dogs or cats and the older residents at the same time. Provide them with a dish each, and let them feed in the same room but at opposite sides. If they are both facing an opposite wall there is no eyeball to eyeball contact and so no challenge. However each can be sure that the other is not getting anything extra special. Their nose will make sure of this. Like us, dining together helps pets to develop friendships, so let them eat at a distance, but within sight and sound.

Supply extra food and water dishes when birds or small mammals meet new companions, this lets the shy ones have a chance of drinking and eating. Birds in particular can be real 'dogs in the manger', if you'll excuse the mixed metaphor, but the 'bottom' bird can starve to death if there is only one seed dish and he is chased away every time he goes near it.

Catflaps: moving can lead to other problems, and one that does crop up is teaching an old cat or even a middle-aged cat for that matter to use a cat

Any cat can learn to use a cat flap if he's given a reward every time he does it right.

door. 'We've moved to the country and thought it would be wonderful for Tiddles being able to come and go as he wished, but he cannot understand how to work the cat door.' Nor would you without some help.

First of all teach the cat to go through the hole in the house door. Take the cat door off, so that there is simply an opening. Feed him after he has entered the house this way. The first time or two might involve a little push through the hole, but if he's hungry the lesson will be learnt by the third time. Then replace the door and wedge it three quarters open, so that the cat gets through with a tiny squeeze. Some doors are spring loaded. If so, adjust the spring to exert the lightest possible pressure. Gradually close the door a bit more each day, and increase the spring pressure so that it takes a harder push each time – and the wind stops blowing through the opening. I'm sure that any cat, no matter how set in his ways, will learn, given the reward of food every time he does it right.

Food left about causes one of the cat-door difficulties. The visiting tom cat that fights, sprays and makes the place smell, has no trouble at all learning how to enter via the cat door. He is not a confused tom cat that does not know that your female is neutered; he is a hungry cat and food is available, so he enters. Cat doors need cats with good feeding manners, ones that eat up so that the plates can be removed. No food, no visiting cats. Simple.

27 · *Wild animals and birds*

Animals or birds taken from the wild should never be kept as pets. That is a generalisation and like all generalisations there are one or two exceptions, but not many.

In the case of British birds, mammals and reptiles the law prohibits keeping some species except by anyone holding a licence from the Department of the Environment. Many aviary-bred British birds may be kept only if they are close rung – that is wearing a sealed ring on their leg. It is only possible to fit such rings to very young birds. The nestling's foot has to be small enough to allow the closed ring to slip over the claws on to the leg. It is also an offence to disturb, or even pick up, some species of British wildlife.

The law is often an ass, and there are some idiotic offences created. If the nesting box that you put in the garden last March is taken down for cleaning and repair on Christmas day, and if there is a blue tit's egg still inside – which has been there since June – it is an offence to blow the egg and keep it for posterity. That seems silly to me. So far as I know, there has never been a prosecution for such an offence, so perhaps the law is a sensible ass. But do beware, and the basic concept that wild things should not be disturbed, is a very sound one.

During May and June every vet sees dozens of small birds, brought to him by caring people, usually children – it's amazing how the numbers increase during the Spring Bank Holiday weekend. They are nearly all young birds fresh from the nest. Some have been badly damaged by a marauding cat, some are naked, eyes hardly open. There is no hope for such as these and a quick death is all that we can offer them. But there are others, almost fully fledged, nearly able to fly. If we (and the birds) are lucky they can be put back in the place they were found and the parent birds will still be about and ready to care for them. The young birds would have been much happier still if they had been left alone in the first place. The greatest help that can be given to any bird that has just left his nest and can hardly fly, is to shut the cat indoors, and keep yourself out of sight. The feathered parents will do the rest.

When winter comes it is nice to feed the birds. They need the food and it makes you feel good and at one with Nature. But do continue once you have started. The worst turn you can do for any bird is to get him into the habit of expecting food each morning, and then failing to supply it one day.

Small birds have a tough time in winter. Because they are small there is a large surface area of bird for a small volume. So heat is easily lost and a lot of food is essential to keep body temperature at a living level. There are only six or seven hours of feeding time on a mid-winter day and every moment must be profitably occupied. If a bird wastes time, waiting for the meal that you provided each day for the last few weeks, he can't regain that time when he's given up hoping. And the other birds have eaten the alternative food anyhow. Don't let them down.

Larger birds and mammals can be helped more effectively than the tinies. Hedgehogs will often learn that the clatter of a saucer means bread and milk is available – although this is not exactly a perfect diet for hedgehogs – but, like whisky, in moderation it does no harm. Canned cat or dog food is better – and they like that too.

Among the large birds, swans would be helped if anglers took more care. There is a hope that lead shot will stop being used as weights on anglers' lines, and this will save many swans from being poisoned by the lead that they eat when searching for gravel to grind the food in the gizzard. Hooks still cause trouble and swans can often be seen with mylon dangling from the beak. There is a fair chance that a hook is on the other end of the nylon. It's astonishing how well a swan can continue to feed when he has a hook stuck in the oesophagus – and how well they recover from operations to remove the hook.

Large birds fly into wires and damage themselves. The extent of the damage varies enormously. A shattered wing may mean destruction, even badly torn skin heals very well. If you should find such a casualty get in touch with the RSPCA, your vet, or the Royal Society for the Protection of Birds who may have a member in the area. Stitching and repairing is often the easy part of the treatment. Nursing and keeping the bird alive while repair takes place is the major problem and needs someone who can devote many hours each day to one bird. That's why there is not always great enthusiasm on the part of a vet or RSPCA inspector to say that they will care for an injured sparrow or robin. It is just impossible to give enough time to care properly, and not giving sufficient attention leads to a delayed death with even more suffering.

Large mammals are injured on the roads. Badgers and foxes in particular. There is a lot of (ill-informed) criticism about the Ministry of Agriculture's policy of trapping and killing badgers which may be carrying tuberculosis. About 1200 badgers are killed each year by men from the Ministry, and more than 1600 dead badgers, killed by motor cars, are handed in by the general public for post mortem by the same Ministry. Many more badgers must be killed by cars and never discovered. I think badger numbers are increasing, but if anything is going to decimate the badger population it is motor cars, not Ministry men. Equally, many more foxes seem to be killed on motorways than are ever killed by the huntsman's hounds.

Injured badgers and foxes are sometimes found by the roadside. Help them if possible, but remember that both can bite. A large sack might make handling easier – if you can get them in the sack in the first place – but a call to the RSPCA could be the better part of valour. Stay with the injured animal until help appears. They can recover from a knock on the head and wander away with nothing worse than a headache. When the vet or inspector arrives to be told that all is well and that he's had a wasted journey, at least he does not have to spend an hour or so trying to find an animal after the caller has left.

Deer are our largest mammal, so shy that it is difficult to believe how many there are. They are counted in thousands rather than dozens. Young fawns often suffer from the help given by people with good intentions when they are found 'abandoned' and 'rescued'. Their mother is entitled to be very indignant. The fawn was left, semi-hidden, mother knew exactly where it was and would have returned at feeding time. But someone interfered.

Don't try to domesticate wild birds or animals. The magpie or jackdaw that is hand-reared either has to spend his life in solitary state or he is 'given his freedom' – he goes free without fear, and is eaten by the first cat that he trusts. Pet foxes grow up into frightened, unsure adults, and the rescued wild rabbit sits waiting for his life to end, in a hutch. Let wild things stay wild. It's tough out there, but that's where they belong.

Useful Addresses

I have tried to preach one message above all others in this book. FIND OUT BEFORE YOU START. The most effective way of finding out about keeping any animal is to talk to those who already do. There are societies concerning any animal you might contemplate keeping – and those you would never dream of getting within a yard of.

Join a society. This list of addresses cannot be complete – new societies emerge all the time – but it might point you in the right direction and towards the enthusiasts that live in your part of the country. Local groups abound. Ask your vet, at the Pet shop, kennels, stables, and library so that you can find out where they meet, and join them.

General addresses
British Veterinary Association
7 Mansfield Street
London W1M 0AT
Phone (01)6366541

PDSA
PDSA House
South Street
Dorking
Surrey
Phone (0306)888291

Guide Dogs for the Blind
Alexander House
9–11 Park Street
Windsor
Berks SL4 1JR
Phone (07535)55711

Universities Federation of Animal Welfare
8 Hamilton Close
South Mimms
Potters Bar
Herts EN6 3QD

RSPCA Headquarters
The Causeway
Horsham
West Sussex RH12 1HG
Phone (0403)64181
(For local branches look under ROYAL, not RSPCA in the telephone directory.)

Dogs
The Kennel Club
1 Clarges Street
Piccadilly
London W1Y 8AB

Dog World (weekly paper)
The Clergy House
The Churchyard
Ashford
Kent TN23 1QW

Our Dogs (weekly paper)
1 Oxford Station Approach
Manchester M60 1SX

Royal College of Veterinary
 Surgeons
32 Belgrave Square
London SW1X 8QP
Phone (01) 2354971

Pet Health Council
4th Floor, Walter House
418–422 The Strand
London WC2R 0PG
Phone (01)8362843

National Canine Defence League
1 & 2 Pratt Mews
London NW1 0AD
Phone (01)3880137

Animal Health Trust
Lanwades Hall
Newmarket
Suffolk CB8 7PN

Cats
Governing Council of the Cat Fancy
4–6 Penel Orlieu
Bridgwater TA6 3PG

Feline Advisory Bureau
350 Upper Richmond Road
Putney
London SW15 6TH
Phone (01)7899553

Cat Protection League
20 North Street
Horsham
West Sussex RH12 1BN

Birds
Budgerigar Society
City house
43 Cliftonville Road
Northampton NN1 5BW
Phone (0604)24549

National Pigeon Association
6 Ryton Road
Boston
Lincolnshire PE21 7QD
Phone (0205)66033

Roller Canary Club
14 Ascension Close
Basingstoke
Phone (0256)27755

Parrot Society
19a De Parys Avenue
Bedford
Phone (0234)58922

Foreign Bird League
Monks Cottage
58 Preston Crow Marsh
Benson
Oxfordshire
Phone (0491)36094

Rabbits
British Rabbits Council
Pure Foy House
7 Kirkgate
Newark
Nottinghamshire
Phone (0636)76042

Guinea pigs
National Cavy Club
9 Parkdale Road
Sheldon
Birmingham B26 3UT

Hamsters
National Hamster Council
4 Beach Mere Rise
Etching Hill
Rugeley
Staffordshire

Gerbils
National Mongolian Gerbil Soc.
4 Langdale Street
Elland
West Yorkshire HX5 0JL
Phone (0422 71005)

Rats
National Fancy Rat Society
55 Effingham Road
Long Ditton, Surbiton
Surrey KT6 4BY
Phone (01)3988304

Fish
Federation of British Aquarists
17 Risborough Road
Maidenhead
Berkshire

Tortoises and Terrapins
British Chelonia Group
105 Burnham Lane
Slough SL1 6LA
Phone (06286)62721

Reptiles and Amphibia
Association for the Study of Reptilia
and Amphibia
Cotswold Wildlife Park
Burford
Oxfordshire
Phone (099382)3006

British Herpetological Society
C/o London Zoo
Regents Park
London NW1 4RY

Insects
Amateur Entomologists Soc.
355 Hounslow Road
Hanworth
Feltham
Middlesex

Hedgehogs
British Hedgehog Preservation
  Society
Knowbury House
Knowbury
Shropshire
(And the RSPCA have a very helpful
leaflet.)

Goats
British Goat Society
Lion House
Rougham
Bury St Edmunds IP30 9LJ
Phone Beyton (0359)70351

Horses
British Horse Society
Stoneleigh
Kenilworth
Warwickshire CV8 2LR
Phone (0359)52241

Donkeys
The Donkey Society
Meadowland
Lower Langham
Dolton
Winkleigh
Devon
Phone (08054)271

Index